**OPPOSING
VIEWPOINTS®
SERIES**

| Educational Equity

Other Books of Related Interest

Opposing Viewpoints Series

America's Changing Demographics
Black Lives Matter
Gender in the 21st Century
Privilege in America
Race in America

At Issue Series

America's Infrastructure
Campus Sexual Violence
Environmental Racism and Classism
Gender Politics
Male Privilege

Current Controversies Series

Freedom of Speech on Campus
Homelessness and Street Crime
Immigration, Asylum, and Sanctuary Cities
LGBTQ Rights
Microaggressions, Safe Spaces, and Trigger Warnings

"Congress shall make no law … abridging the freedom of speech, or of the press."

First Amendment to the US Constitution

The basic foundation of our democracy is the First Amendment guarantee of freedom of expression. The Opposing Viewpoints series is dedicated to the concept of this basic freedom and the idea that it is more important to practice it than to enshrine it.

OPPOSING VIEWPOINTS® SERIES

| Educational Equity

M. M. Eboch, Book Editor

GREENHAVEN
PUBLISHING

#1268122282

Published in 2022 by Greenhaven Publishing, LLC
353 3rd Avenue, Suite 255, New York, NY 10010

Copyright © 2022 by Greenhaven Publishing, LLC

First Edition

Articles in Greenhaven Publishing anthologies are often edited for length to meet page requirements. In addition, original titles of these works are changed to clearly present the main thesis and to explicitly indicate the author's opinion. Every effort is made to ensure that Greenhaven Publishing accurately reflects the original intent of the authors. Every effort has been made to trace the owners of the copyrighted material.

Cover image: Monkey Business Image/Shutterstock.com

Library of Congress Cataloging-in-Publication Data
Names: Eboch, M. M. editor.
Title: Educational equity / M. M. Eboch, Editor.
Other titles: Educational equity (Greenhaven Publishing)
Description: First edition. | New York : Greenhaven Publishing, 2022. |
  Series: Opposing viewpoints | Includes bibliographical references and
  index. | Summary: "Anthology of essays exploring parity in education"--
  Provided by publisher.
Identifiers: LCCN 2021037203 | ISBN 9781534508453 (library binding) | ISBN
  9781534508446 (paperback)
Subjects: LCSH: Educational equalization--United States. |
  Education--Social aspects--United States. | Education--United
  States--History. | Sexism in education--United States. | Racism in
  education--United States. | Students with social
  disabilities--Education.
Classification: LCC LC213 .E393 2022 | DDC 379.2/60973--dc23
LC record available at https://lccn.loc.gov/2021037203

Manufactured in the United States of America

Website: http://greenhavenpublishing.com

Contents

Chapter 5: How Can Educational Equity Be Achieved?

The Importance of Opposing Viewpoints

Perhaps every generation experiences a period in time in which the populace seems especially polarized, starkly divided on the important issues of the day and gravitating toward the far ends of the political spectrum and away from a consensus-facilitating middle ground. The world that today's students are growing up in and that they will soon enter into as active and engaged citizens is deeply fragmented in just this way. Issues relating to terrorism, immigration, women's rights, minority rights, race relations, health care, taxation, wealth and poverty, the environment, policing, military intervention, the proper role of government—in some ways, perennial issues that are freshly and uniquely urgent and vital with each new generation—are currently roiling the world.

If we are to foster a knowledgeable, responsible, active, and engaged citizenry among today's youth, we must provide them with the intellectual, interpretive, and critical-thinking tools and experience necessary to make sense of the world around them and of the all-important debates and arguments that inform it. After all, the outcome of these debates will in large measure determine the future course, prospects, and outcomes of the world and its peoples, particularly its youth. If they are to become successful members of society and productive and informed citizens, students need to learn how to evaluate the strengths and weaknesses of someone else's arguments, how to sift fact from opinion and fallacy, and how to test the relative merits and validity of their own opinions against the known facts and the best possible available information. The landmark series Opposing Viewpoints has been providing students with just such critical-thinking skills and exposure to the debates surrounding society's most urgent contemporary issues for many years, and it continues to serve this essential role with undiminished commitment, care, and rigor.

The key to the series's success in achieving its goal of sharpening students' critical-thinking and analytic skills resides in its title—

Opposing Viewpoints. In every intriguing, compelling, and engaging volume of this series, readers are presented with the widest possible spectrum of distinct viewpoints, expert opinions, and informed argumentation and commentary, supplied by some of today's leading academics, thinkers, analysts, politicians, policy makers, economists, activists, change agents, and advocates. Every opinion and argument anthologized here is presented objectively and accorded respect. There is no editorializing in any introductory text or in the arrangement and order of the pieces. No piece is included as a "straw man," an easy ideological target for cheap point-scoring. As wide and inclusive a range of viewpoints as possible is offered, with no privileging of one particular political ideology or cultural perspective over another. It is left to each individual reader to evaluate the relative merits of each argument—as he or she sees it, and with the use of ever-growing critical-thinking skills—and grapple with his or her own assumptions, beliefs, and perspectives to determine how convincing or successful any given argument is and how the reader's own stance on the issue may be modified or altered in response to it.

This process is facilitated and supported by volume, chapter, and selection introductions that provide readers with the essential context they need to begin engaging with the spotlighted issues, with the debates surrounding them, and with their own perhaps shifting or nascent opinions on them. In addition, guided reading and discussion questions encourage readers to determine the authors' point of view and purpose, interrogate and analyze the various arguments and their rhetoric and structure, evaluate the arguments' strengths and weaknesses, test their claims against available facts and evidence, judge the validity of the reasoning, and bring into clearer, sharper focus the reader's own beliefs and conclusions and how they may differ from or align with those in the collection or those of their classmates.

Research has shown that reading comprehension skills improve dramatically when students are provided with compelling, intriguing, and relevant "discussable" texts. The subject matter of these collections could not be more compelling, intriguing, or urgently relevant to today's students and the world they are poised to inherit. The anthologized articles and the reading and discussion questions that are included with them also provide the basis for stimulating, lively, and passionate classroom debates. Students who are compelled to anticipate objections to their own argument and identify the flaws in those of an opponent read more carefully, think more critically, and steep themselves in relevant context, facts, and information more thoroughly. In short, using discussable text of the kind provided by every single volume in the Opposing Viewpoints series encourages close reading, facilitates reading comprehension, fosters research, strengthens critical thinking, and greatly enlivens and energizes classroom discussion and participation. The entire learning process is deepened, extended, and strengthened.

For all of these reasons, Opposing Viewpoints continues to be exactly the right resource at exactly the right time—when we most need to provide readers with the critical-thinking tools and skills that will not only serve them well in school but also in their careers and their daily lives as decision-making family members, community members, and citizens. This series encourages respectful engagement with and analysis of opposing viewpoints and fosters a resulting increase in the strength and rigor of one's own opinions and stances. As such, it helps make readers "future ready," and that readiness will pay rich dividends for the readers themselves, for the citizenry, for our society, and for the world at large.

Introduction

> *"All too often, we rely on band-aid approaches in which another new literacy or math intervention is introduced to decrease the achievement gap. ... It's time to push through these 'quick fixes' and move into intentional systems change work."[1]*

Today, most people agree in principle at least that everyone should have equal opportunities in education. Educational opportunities are important because they better prepare people for success in life. A higher level of education is associated with higher earnings throughout life, better health, and more life satisfaction. In short, educated people are wealthier and healthier. Educating individuals also benefits society. The economy benefits from knowledgeable and skilled workers. Democratic society needs citizens who can understand and participate in government.

Because of these benefits, the United States and many other countries provide free education to all children for a number of years. Children are required to attend school or receive schooling at home. State laws determine when a student must start school, and when they are allowed to leave.

This was not always the case. In 1852, Massachusetts became the first US state to require every city and town to offer a primary school and to require parents to send their children to those schools. Mississippi was the last state to pass a law requiring school attendance, which it did in 1917. Throughout US history, the educational system favored white males. Before the compulsory schooling laws, most girls at best learned basic reading and writing skills, along with homemaking skills. Girls from upper class families might also learn dance, music, and French so they could attract suitors. During the nineteenth century, women educators began to encourage better education for women. This still meant a focus on domestic skills along with literacy and moral training. Few careers were open to women beyond teaching. Women were not allowed to attend men's colleges, but some colleges for women opened starting in the 1830s.

By the early twentieth century, most high schools and colleges had become coeducational, open to boys and girls. For the first half of the century, many classrooms were segregated by sex. While boys were encouraged to take advanced math and science classes, girls were discouraged or even prevented from taking those classes. They were required to take home economics or domestic science and often encouraged into a vocational track that might prepare them for a job as a secretary or clerical worker. In 1972, Title IX addressed sex-based discrimination. The legislation prohibited discrimination based on sex in schools that received federal funds. Title IX has mainly been used to attack discrimination in athletics and athletic scholarships, but the law also covers discrimination in academics. The Women's Educational Equity Act (WEEA) of 1974 helped schools recruit girls for math, science, and athletic programs. However, funding for WEEA was drastically cut in the 1980s.

People of color faced even more discrimination, as they were often not allowed to attend the same schools as white students. Their segregated schools typically received less funding and provided a poorer education than the schools for white students. In 1955, the Supreme Court ruled that these separate schools could not be equal and demanded schools be integrated "with all deliberate speed." However, it took until the 1980s for the federal courts to fully eliminate legalized segregation in schools. Even today, schools remain heavily segregated by race and ethnicity. More than seven in ten black students attend a high-poverty school, according to the Economic Policy Institute. Less than one in three white students attend a high poverty school.

Even when people agree that everyone deserves a good education and equal opportunities, making sure everyone gets the same opportunities is a challenge. Educational experts have shifted from focusing on equality in education to equity in education. Equality treats everyone the same. In education, equality would mean every student has the same access to the same education, regardless of their race, sex, background, or other factors. Equality holds all students to the same standards and objectives, regardless of their abilities or circumstances.

Equity, on the other hand, recognizes that students don't start in the same place. Some students need different resources to achieve the same goals as their peers. A student with a physical disability may require physical assistance. A student with dyslexia may need books on tape and more time for tests. A student who is learning English as a second language may need different support than someone who grew up speaking English. Equity acknowledges that every person has different needs. It suggests people should get the support they need to do their best. That support may be different from what their peers need. While equity is an admirable goal, it is not easy to achieve. The US public educational system was built around standardization. Every student is given the same goals and expectations. Teachers are told to develop their lessons around standards adopted by the states. Students are judged with standardized tests. A standardized education can be equal, but it is often not equitable.

Opposing Viewpoints: Educational Equity examines these issues in chapters titled "How Does Educational Equity Impact Society?"; "How Does Gender Impact Educational Opportunities?"; "How Does Racial Discrimination Lead to Inequities in Education?"; "How Does Socioeconomic Status Lead to Differences in Learning?"; and "How Can Educational Equity Be Achieved?". Viewpoint authors explore the complicated issues inherent in the US education system today. Understanding and addressing these important issues is key to making sure every student achieves their best.

Notes

1. Jen Neitzel, Ph.D., "The Hard Work of Equity," Educational Equity Institute, https://educationalequityinstitute.com/the-hard-work-of-second-generation-equity/.

OPPOSING
VIEWPOINTS®
SERIES

CHAPTER 1

How Does Educational Equity Impact Society?

Chapter Preface

What is equality? What is equity? How do they apply to education?

Theories about education change regularly. Even when schools, communities, and the government agree on goals, they may not agree on how to reach those goals. Many schools and teachers continue to do things the way they have been done for years, but some schools try different methods to see what succeeds. In order to fully judge what works and what doesn't, studies must track the results of these experiments. Only then can educational experts determine the best practices for schools.

One change in recent years has been a move from equality to equity. In education, equality would mean treating every student the same. For a long time, this was the goal of most educational systems. Most people believed that giving every student the same opportunity would allow the best students to succeed. If students failed, they were seen to be at fault.

However, now educational experts recognize that students do not all start in the same place. Giving them exactly the same resources and support will not allow all students to achieve their best. Equity acknowledges that students come from different backgrounds and have different physical, mental, and emotional strengths and weaknesses. Equity attempts to help every individual reach their fullest potential by giving them the specific support they need.

Achieving equity isn't easy. It means systems must be in place to address many factors. Some students live in temporary shelters or on the streets or do not feel safe at home. Some students do not have access to basic healthcare. Some have mental health issues, learning challenges, or physical disabilities. Some do not have computers, Internet access, or even electricity at home. Some students are not fluent in English. Addressing all of these challenges may seem daunting, but promoting equity in education has many benefits. At equitable schools, students learn better, which leads to better job opportunities. That in turn leads to more job satisfaction and better earnings throughout life. Educational equity also helps people lead healthier lives.

Educational equity also benefits communities, the country, and the world. Equity leads to economic growth and helps people make better decisions as voters and citizens. It even helps individuals become more compassionate, which is good for society.

The viewpoints in this chapter explore the differences between equality and equity as the start of an exploration into how schools can achieve fairness and inclusion.

> *"The route to achieving equity will not be accomplished through treating everyone equally."*

Schools Need Equity, Not Equality

Waterford

In the following viewpoint, authors at Waterford explain the difference between equality and equity and how the terms apply to education. The authors note that some schools assume students all have the same advantages, so treating them equally is fair. However, at most schools, students come from different backgrounds and have different needs. The viewpoint lists challenges to classroom equity and then notes benefits to promoting equity. Students do better in school, are healthier, and have more opportunities in the future. In addition, the school and even the community benefits. Waterford is an organization dedicated to promoting excellence and equity in education.

As you read, consider the following questions:

1. What is equity in education?
2. How is equity different from equality?
3. What are some benefits to promoting equity in education?

The quality of education that students receive directly correlates to their quality of life years down the road.[1] Early education

"Why Understanding Equity vs Equality in Schools Can Help You Create an Inclusive Classroom," Waterford, May 2, 2020. Reprinted by permission.

in particular has the power to shape a child's future and the more resources available to them, the better. For this reason, it's crucial for educators to address any barriers young students face to succeeding in school.

The key is equity. Equity means offering individualized support to students that addresses possible barriers, like poverty or limited transportation. 97% of teachers agree that equity is important, but many don't know how to best work towards it in their classrooms.[2] But once educators have the right strategies to promote equity in schools, they can make sure each student is prepared to reach their potential.

Want to create inclusive and equitable classrooms at your school? Discover the difference between equity and equality, then learn five strategies for resolving common barriers to equity in education.

Main Differences Between Equity and Equality

When it comes to equity vs equality in education, the terms are often used interchangeably.[3] But understanding the distinction between the two is essential for resolving issues faced by disadvantaged students in the classroom. While working towards equity and equality can both do good, equity should be an educator's end goal. The reason lies in the difference between being fair vs equal.

Equality is more commonly associated with social issues, perhaps because more people know what it means. In a nutshell, its definition is as it sounds–the state of being equal. When a group focuses on equality, everyone has the same rights, opportunities, and resources.[4] Equality is beneficial, but it often doesn't address specific needs. Giving each student a take-home laptop, for example, would not address students who don't have Internet in their houses. Even if a school is equal, some students may still struggle.

Equity, on the other hand, provides people with resources that fit their circumstances. The World Health Organization (WHO) definition of social equity is "the absence of avoidable or remediable differences among groups of people."[5] Schools that prioritize equity versus equality are more in tune to their students' needs and provide resources to overcome their specific challenges.

In short, equality is:

- Generic
- Group-focused
- Equal

And equity is:

- Adaptable
- Individual-focused
- Fair

"The route to achieving equity will not be accomplished through treating everyone equally," says the Race Matters Institute. "It will be achieved by treating everyone equitably, or justly according to their circumstances."[6] Equity is more thoughtful and, while it's harder work, it is better at resolving disadvantages. While equality is an admirable goal, try shifting your school's focus to equity for a more effective outcome.

A CRUCIAL DIFFERENCE IN PEDAGOGY

Between 2009 and 2018, several federal initiatives were rolled out in the interest of bridging academic inequity. Here are a few examples:

Title I: This formula grant program provides financial assistance to local education agencies (LEAs) and schools with high numbers or high percentages of children from low-income households to ensure that the students meet challenging state standards.

IDEA: The Individuals with Disabilities Education Act of 2004 (IDEA) "authorizes formula grants to states and discretionary grants to institutions of higher education and other nonprofit organizations to support research, demonstrations, technical assistant and dissemination, technology, and personnel development and parent-training and information centers."

Challenges Involving Equity and Equality in Schools

Barriers to an inclusive education can affect groups based on race, gender, and many other factors. The issues are not only who is being targeted but also how we try to resolve them. In terms of equity vs equality in the classroom, most schools focus on horizontal equity. The definition of horizontal equity in education is treating people who are already assumed equal in the same way.[7]

Horizontal equity is only useful in homogenous schools, where each person really is given the same opportunities in life. But in most schools, students will come from a variety of backgrounds–some more privileged than others. For this reason, educators should focus on vertical equity, which assumes that students have different needs and provides individual resources based on said needs.[8]

Another challenge facing equity vs equality in education is poverty. 60% of the most disadvantaged students come from low-income homes or communities.[9] Because their families or schools might have very limited budgets, it can be difficult to provide these students with equitable resources. Additionally, these at-risk communities often have trouble keeping educators who can

Promise Neighborhoods: This discretionary and competitive grant program provides funding to support nonprofit organizations, including faith-based nonprofits, institutions of higher education, and Indian tribes in order to give all children growing up in "promise neighborhoods" access to great schools and community support.

Investing in Innovation: This grant program provides funding "to support LEAs and nonprofit organizations in partnership with one or more LEAs or a consortium of schools." The grants are set to be awarded to schools with a record of improving student achievement and attainment with innovative practices, among other qualifications.

"Equality vs. Equity: A Crucial Difference in Pedagogy," King University Online, April 20, 2018.

make a difference: 62% of high-poverty schools report that it is challenging to retain high-quality teachers.[10]

According to the Scholastic Teachers and Principals Report, these are a few additional barriers to equity in American schools:[11]

- Family crises
- Mental health issues
- Lack of healthcare
- Coming to school hungry
- Homelessness or living in a temporary shelter
- Still learning the English language

Recognizing the challenges preventing equity in your classroom is the first step to resolving them. Try to analyze any issues that are keeping your students from succeeding in school. Perhaps you teach in a low-income community, or one of your students is an English language learner (ELL). By evaluating the needs of individual students, you're much closer to providing them with the support necessary for academic achievement.

Benefits of Focusing on Equity in Education

Equity in schools is the answer to supporting every student, not just those from disadvantaged backgrounds. When schools provide their students with resources that fit individual circumstances, the entire classroom environment improves.[12] Not only that, but the importance of equity extends to our society as a whole. In equitable communities, everyone has the opportunity to succeed regardless of their original circumstances.

On a surface level, the benefits of inclusive and equitable classrooms extend to academic achievement. Schools with the smallest achievement gaps between demographics have the highest overall test scores.[13] This means that when the most disadvantaged student scores improve, students from more privileged backgrounds improve, too. When schools are mindful of different backgrounds and provide the right resources, all students are prepared to learn and help each other succeed.

Equity can also strengthen a student's health and social-emotional development. In a study involving over 4,300 students in Southern California, the children who felt safer, less lonely, and reported less bullying also had higher diversity levels in their classes.[14] Being equipped to promote diversity and provide for students from all backgrounds makes for an environment where students feel comfortable and have better emotional regulation. Additionally, equitable communities are linked to better health and longer average lifespans.[15]

Surrounding communities benefit from equity in schools as well. Equity is linked to stronger social cohesion, meaning that individuals connect with each other better and are more compassionate.[16] It also leads to long-term economic growth.[17] This means that promoting equity in schools can be one of the best and most effective social investments.

To summarize, these are some of the benefits of focusing on equity in education:

- Higher test scores
- Better health
- Stronger social atmosphere
- Longer life
- Economic growth

Tips for Using Equity to Create an Inclusive Classroom

Knowing the difference between equity and equality is the first step to creating a classroom where every child can succeed. From there, educators can take steps to better address the challenges faced by struggling students.

Keep these five tips in mind for promoting equity in your classroom and helping every student succeed:

- Remember that every child is different and has unique needs. Evaluate any challenges that students face and, if needed, offer support or resources [18]

- Cultivate an environment in your classroom where every student feels heard. Encourage them to speak out against unfairness and let you know if they're facing any hardships at home or in class
- Parent engagement is a particularly helpful way to resolve challenges involving equity. Keep open communication with parents and encourage them to volunteer or attend school events to involve them with their child's education [19]
- Provide equity training in schools for faculty members so teachers know how to resolve common barriers [20]
- Add diversity and inclusion activities as well as lessons against prejudice to your school curriculum so every student feels like they belong [21]

Endnotes

1. OECD Observer Staff. Ten Steps to Equity in Education. Organization for Economic Co-operation and Development, January 2008, pp. 1-8.
2. Scholastic Team. Barriers to Equity in Education | Teachers and Principals School Report. Retrieved from scholastic.com: http://www.scholastic.com/teacherprincipalreport/barriers-to-equity.htm.
3. Winston-Salem State University. Strategic Planning at Winston-Salem State University: Working Toward Equity. Retrieved from wssu.edu: https://www.wssu.edu/strategic-plan/documents/a-summary-of-equity-vs-equality.pdf.
4. Just Health Action. Part 1: Introduction to Environmental Justice, Equity, and Health. Retrieved from justhealthaction.org: http://justhealthaction.org/wp-content/uploads/2010/05/JHA-Lesson-Plan-3-How-are-equity-and-equality-different-final.pdf.
5. World Health Organization. WHO | Equity. Retrieved from who.int: https://www.who.int/healthsystems/topics/equity/en/.
6. Race Matters Institute. Racial Equality or Racial Equity? The Difference it Makes. Retrieved from viablefuturescenture.org: https://viablefuturescenter.org/racemattersinstitute/2014/04/02/racial-equality-or-racial-equity-the-difference-it-makes/.
7. Catapano, J. The Challenges of Equity in Public Education. Retrieved from teachhub.com: https://www.teachhub.com/challenges-equity-public-education
8. Ibid.
9. OECD Observer Staff. Ten Steps to Equity in Education. Organization for Economic Co-operation and Development, January 2008, pp. 1-8.
10. Ibid.
11. Scholastic Team. Barriers to Equity in Education | Teachers and Principals School Report. Retrieved from scholastic.com: http://www.scholastic.com/teacherprincipalreport/barriers-to-equity.htm.

12. OECD Observer Staff. Ten Steps to Equity in Education. Organization for Economic Co-operation and Development, January 2008, pp. 1-8.
13. Gorard, S., and Smith, E. An international comparison of equity in education systems. School Comparative Education, 2004, 40(1), pp. 15-28.
14. Atchison, B., Diffey, L., Rafa, A., and Sarubbi, M. Equity in Education: Key Questions to Consider. Education Commission of the States, June, 2017, pp. 1-6.
15. OECD Observer Staff. Ten Steps to Equity in Education. Organization for Economic Co-operation and Development, January 2008, pp. 1-8.
16. Ibid.
17. Ibid.
18. Scholastic Team. Barriers to Equity in Education | Teachers and Principals School Report. Retrieved from scholastic.com: http://www.scholastic.com/ teacherprincipalreport/barriers-to-equity.htm.
19. OECD Observer Staff. Ten Steps to Equity in Education. Organization for Economic Co-operation and Development, January 2008, pp. 1-8.
20. Atchison, B., Diffey, L., Rafa, A., and Sarubbi, M. Equity in Education: Key Questions to Consider. Education Commission of the States, June, 2017, pp. 1-6.
21. OECD Observer Staff. Ten Steps to Equity in Education. Organization for Economic Co-operation and Development, January 2008, pp. 1-8.

"ESEA was passed with the intention of bridging a clear gap between children in poverty and those from privilege."

The Federal Role in Education Has a Long History

Dustin Hornbeck

In the following viewpoint, written in the early stages of the Trump administration, Dustin Hornbeck runs through the history of public education in the United States and traces the fluctuating role of the federal government in education. Historically, public education was the purview of the states, but that changed in the mid-twentieth century, when the federal government became more involved. Since then, there has been some debate about whether education should be the business of state governments or national governments. In his first year, President Trump pledged to scale back the federal government's role, which the author argues could have negative impacts on certain students and their communities. Dustin Hornbeck is a postdoctoral research fellow of educational leadership and policy at the University of Texas Arlington.

As you read, consider the following questions:

1. In what year did the US Department of Education become a cabinet-level agency?
2. What was the first US state to require free education?
3. Specifically how did the ESEA change education in the United States?

President Donald Trump has directed the United States Department of Education to evaluate whether the federal government has "overstepped its legal authority" in the field of education. This is not a new issue in American politics.

Ever since the Department of Education became a Cabinet-level agency in 1979, opposition to federalized education has been a popular rallying cry among conservatives. Ronald Reagan advocated to dismantle the department while campaigning for his presidency, and many others since then have called for more power to be put back into the states' hands when it comes to educational policy. In February of this year, legislation was introduced to eliminate the Department of Education entirely.

So, what is the role of the state versus the federal government in the world of K-12 education?

As a researcher of education policy and politics, I have seen that people are divided on the role that the federal government should play in K-12 education—a role that has changed over the course of history.

Growth of Public Education in States

The 10th Amendment to the United States Constitution states:

> The powers not delegated to the United States by the Constitution, nor prohibited by it to the States, are reserved to the States respectively, or to the people.

This leaves the power to create schools and a system for education in the hands of individual states, rather than the central national government. Today, all 50 states provide public schooling to their young people—with 50 approaches to education within the borders of one nation.

Public schooling on a state level began in 1790, when Pennsylvania became the first state to require free education. This service was extended only to poor families, assuming that wealthy people could afford to pay for their own education. New York followed suit in 1805. In 1820, Massachusetts was the first state to have a tuition-free high school for all, and also the first to require compulsory education.

By the late 1800s, public education had spread to most states, in a movement often referred to as the common school movement. After World War I, urban populations swelled, and vocational education and secondary education became part of the American landscape. By 1930, every state had some sort of compulsory education law. This led to increased control of schools by cities and states.

Federal Role in Education

As for the federal government's role, education is not specifically addressed in the Constitution, but a historical precedent of central government involvement does exist.

In 1787, the Continental Congress, the central government of the United States between 1776 and 1787, passed the Northwest Ordinance, which became the governing document for Ohio, Illinois, Indiana, Michigan, Wisconsin and part of Minnesota.

The ordinance included a provision encouraging the creation of schools as a key component of "good government and the happiness of mankind." Just two years earlier, the Land Ordinance of 1785 required land to be reserved in townships for the building of schools.

The role of the federal government in general grew much larger after the Great Depression and World War II, but this growth largely excluded K-12 educationuntil the 1960s. In 1964,

President Lyndon B. Johnson included education policy in his vision of a "Great Society."

Elementary and Secondary Education Act

In 1965, President Johnson signed the Elementary and Secondary Education Act (ESEA) into law. This law decidedly changed the role of the federal government in the world of K-12 education.

ESEA doubled the amount of federal expenditures for K-12 education, worked to change the relationship between states and the central government in the education arena, called for equal treatment of students no matter where they reside and attempted to improve reading and math competency for children in poverty.

ESEA was passed with the intention of bridging a clear gap between children in poverty and those from privilege. Title I of the ESEA, which is still referenced frequently in K-12 education policy, is a major provision of the bill, which distributed federal funding to districts with low-income families.

ESEA today

ESEA is still the law of the United States today. However, the law has required periodic reauthorization, which has led to significant changes since 1965. One of the most well-known reauthorizations was President George W. Bush's No Child Left Behind (NCLB) Act of 2001. NCLB called for 100 percent proficiency in math and reading scores nationwide by 2014, and expanded the role of standardized testing to measure student achievement.

Under President Barack Obama, Race to the Top was established, requiring states to compete for federal grants through a point system, which rewarded certain educational policies and achievements. This resulted in nationwide changes in the way teachers are evaluated, and placed even more emphasis on test results.

In 2015, Obama signed the Every Student Succeeds Act (ESSA) into law. This is the latest reauthorization of ESEA, and returns some federal power over education back to states, including evaluation measures and teacher quality standards.

The Debate Continues

Since the 1980s, a growing trend in the field of K-12 education has been the growth of school choice and charter schools. Every state has its own policy regarding these issues, but during the presidential campaign of 2016, President Trump assured that his administration would provide federal money to help students attend a school of their choice. Secretary of Education Betsy DeVos has dedicated her career to the cause of school choice.

On April 26, President Trump signed the "Education Federalism Executive Order," which requires the United States Department of Education to spend 300 days evaluating the role of the federal government in education. The purpose of the order is to "determine where the Federal Government has unlawfully overstepped state and local control." This comes on the back of a proposed 13.5 percent cut to the national education budget.

It's not yet known what the results of this study might conclude. But, in my opinion, it may impact ESEA and the current funding structure that has been the norm for over 50 years, dramatically impacting funding for students in poverty and with special needs.

| "Once the school reopening question is settled, we will be left with the consequences of this pandemic—the learning loss, the economic recession, the racial and economic disparities."

The Pandemic Might Have Changed the Fate of Our Public Education System

Didi Kuo

In the following viewpoint Didi Kuo argues that the COVID-19 pandemic has potentially caused some long-term shifts in the United States public schools. Parents who have the means and the interest in avoiding future situations involving remote learning can simply exit the system, turning instead to private tutors, learning pods, and even private schools. If that were to happen on a larger scale, it would hurt the public schools, which depend on student counts for funding and other resources. Ultimately, students of lower socioeconomic status would suffer. Didi Kuo is a senior research scholar at the Center on Democracy, Development, and the Rule of Law at the Freeman-Sogli Institute for International Studies at Stanford University.

"The Politics of Post-Pandemic Education," by Didi Kuo, Niskanen Center, April 8, 2021, https://www.niskanencenter.org/the-politics-of-post-pandemic-education/. Licensed under CC BY 4.0 International.

As you read, consider the following questions:

1. According to the viewpoint, how did the pandemic change traditional alliances?
2. What did George W. Bush's education secretary call a "terrorist organization"?
3. How could the pandemic hurt public schools and their students?

Spring break usually means a giddy escape from the classroom for children across America. This year, however, the millions of students who have not set foot in a classroom since last spring are celebrating by closing their laptops for a few days. Many of these students have no prospect of returning to class anytime soon—and their pandemic-shuttered schools have become the focus of an ugly battle among teachers' unions, school boards, parents, and elected officials about how, and when, they should reopen. As the politics of reopening have grown increasingly antagonistic and personal,[1] the pandemic is blurring partisan and racial cleavages around public education and creating new coalitions that could remain powerful players in local education politics. At stake is the fate of our public education system itself.

This shift may seem surprising because for much of the past 40 years, the politics of education have remained largely consistent: school boards are locally elected (often by voters who do not represent the parents or students)[2] and teachers' unions advocate for teachers and schools. Parents, in turn, traditionally are united with unions in any number of causes. Teachers' unions secure resources and funding for schools; parent-teacher associations organize within schools to help. Labor activism among teachers has led to high-profile strikes across the country. In what became the "Red for Ed" campaigns of 2017-18, teachers in both Democratic and Republican states (including not just California but also West Virginia, Arizona, Oklahoma, and Kentucky) demanded better pay and conditions.[3] Public support for teachers and teachers' unions has remained high, although opinion data shows that parents are mixed on whether or not they think unions improve the quality of education.[4]

With millions of children out of school for more than a year, however, traditional alliances are being scrambled. On the West Coast, for example, teachers have been offered priority vaccinations, facility improvements, and hazard pay, but unions are still refusing to return to classrooms and in many cases are embroiled in conflict with their districts. Centers for Disease Control and Prevention recommendations and evidence from private and public schools that are operating in person indicate that schools can be (and have been) safe environments. Even so, many districts have been slow to develop reopening plans, provoking the ire of parents.[5] School boards, in turn, have come under fire for their lack of planning and their demonization of parents.[6] And parents are fleeing public schools, with private school applications up in urban areas.[7] The fissures have highlighted the basic collective action problem underlying the politics of public education: While there are well-organized interests in favor of educators (i.e., teachers' unions), there is no organization of diffuse "pro-good-schools" or "pro-student interests.

The lack of such a constituency may be unsurprising: Public education is a guaranteed public good that no one needs to lobby to receive; most states require the enrollment of children in school until the age of 16. But like all distributive goods, education is not equally distributed. And thus the constituencies that have emerged around education do not argue in favor of educational resources generally—"quality instruction," "better schools." Instead, constituencies tend to organize around racial or wealth lines, with white and suburban parents better able to secure scarce educational resources for their schools and children. Those parents who do get involved in school politics might advocate for things like gifted and talented programs, rather than structural change that would advance the interests of all students.[8] Those who take up the reform cause—advocating for greater accountability, or for school choice—do not typically have the political backing or organizational heft of the most powerful actor in education policy, the teachers' unions.

While these unions are often unfairly maligned—George W. Bush's education secretary, Rod Paige, famously called one of them a "terrorist organization"—their ability to stop even widely popular initiatives that they oppose is quite real. School openings themselves are the perfect case in point. In a recent paper, political scientists Michael Hartney and Leslie Finger found that political variables, rather than COVID-related factors, were the most significant determinants of whether or not districts adopted in-person or remote education last fall.[9] Strong Democratic support and strong teachers' unions were the strongest predictors of districts abandoning in-person reopening plans. Districts with greater numbers of Catholic schools were more likely to consider in-person options—likely because parents had non-union, in-person options at the start of the year. And as the school year has progressed, reopening has been mired in political standoffs with teachers' unions at their center.

Despite the appearance of parental organization today, parents are "not a well-organized interest and never have been," according to Stanford University's Terry Moe.[10] When California adopted a so-called parent trigger law in 2010 to allow parents to take action against the administrators of underperforming schools, few parents availed themselves of it. Most parents are allies of their schools and teachers. As Ohio State's Vladimir Kogan points out, parents (particularly progressives) may also attach expressive value to being part of the public school system.

There are two likely paths forward for parents and public education. The first is that the parents most fed up with remote schooling will simply exit. It could be what Michael Hartney describes as "invisible exit"—supplementing their children's education with tutors and learning pods, for example.[11] It could also be a visible exit to private schools—an option that helps the tiny sliver of kids in private schools and that hurts, directly and indirectly, the many more kids in the public education system.

The second option is that the barriers around what were once politically untenable options for Democrats will begin to break down. The accountability movement and charter schools have, at various times in the past, enjoyed bipartisan support; but of late, Democratic politicians have aligned themselves with teachers' unions that oppose both high-stakes testing requirements and charters. These are recent, and tenuous, political arrangements. Parents may now be more open to school choice or may try to attract resources from philanthropists interested in investing in different educational models.

What is not likely, according to education experts, is any kind of lasting political coalition backing students' interests. Teachers' unions are powerful political actors in part because they are entrenched and well-resourced, but also because of the structural power dynamics at play in education itself. Unlike the private sector, where union power is dwarfed by corporate power, teachers face no organized political opposition. The stark divergence in parents' and unions' preferences over reopening is unlikely to emerge in a similar fashion in the future. But nonetheless, there can be lessons learned—about the vital function of our schools and the need for powerful actors across the political spectrum to invest more in and care more about our nation's children.

Exit from Public Schools

Debates about schooling affect the 56 million children enrolled in the nation's public schools; nine out of every 10 kids go through the public education system.[12] Exempt from these debates are the 5.5 million children who attend private schools, which include both parochial/religious schools and nonsectarian schools. Private schools are less racially diverse than public schools, enrolling far more white students (67 percent compared to 48 percent white students in public schools) than Black or Latino students. Perhaps obviously, private school parents do not attend local school board meetings or join public school PTAs.

Parents whose kids are in private schools are also buying the privilege of not having to worry about what schools are like for the vast majority of American kids. In a recent article in The Atlantic, Caitlin Flanagan described the exorbitant wealth and demands of parents in independent schools, which serve as pipelines of affluence and privilege.[13] While only 2 percent of American students attend independent schools, 24 to 29 percent of students at universities like Yale, Princeton, Brown, and Dartmouth come from such schools. Although not all private schools are this selective and well-endowed, it is nonetheless worth considering the radical counterfactual of a society in which all parental educational investments went into public, rather than private, schools. The New York Times' Nikole Hannah-Jones has written that "democracy works only if those who have the money or the power to opt out of public things choose instead to opt in for the common good."[14]

School closures are only likely to speed up private school enrollments. In cities like San Francisco and Washington, D.C., private school applications are up and public school enrollments are down. Declining public school enrollments mean less funding for districts, since funding is allocated according to a "butts in seats" formula. Some of these public-to-private parents might be like the white and suburban parents who only advocate for what advances their own children's interests. But some might be the progressive parents who were staunch advocates of public education or the squeaky wheels who devoted time to educational advocacy—maybe not always successfully, but still. It is an open question whether the public schools are better off without them.

Shifting Coalitions and the Education Reform Movement

The reopening battles are also likely to shift the political coalitions behind teachers' unions on the one hand and reform advocates on the other. Democrats who have long supported unions now find themselves working at odds with them: President Joe Biden and Secretary of Education Miguel Cardona (a champion of teachers' unions) have been vocal about the need to reopen schools, as have Democratic governors and mayors. The early politicization of the pandemic has been difficult to shake, but the left-leaning publication The Nation is now writing in favor of reopenings[15] and Republican candidates are campaigning against suburban Democratic representatives on the issue of school closures.[16]

As Hartney explained, the reaction to President Donald Trump and Secretary of Education Betsy DeVos helped align Democratic interests with teachers' unions and against high-stakes testing and school choice. But as Democratic politicians now take on the unions, public sentiment is also shifting. This could lead parents (particularly in urban districts) to take the education reform movement more seriously. Black and Latino parents have long supported school choice, vouchers, and charter schools at higher rates than white parents: in 2019, a poll by Harvard researchers found that 70 percent of Black Democrats supported targeted school vouchers and 55 percent supported charter schools, compared to only 40 percent of white parents supporting targeted vouchers and 33 percent supporting charters. Charter schools, which are publicly funded and privately managed, constitute around 7 percent of public schools and enroll some 3 million students.[17] Charter schools have higher rates of Black (26 percent) and Latino (33 percent) students than noncharter public schools (15 percent Black and 27 percent Latino).[18]

Once the school reopening question is settled, we will be left with the consequences of this pandemic — the learning loss, the economic recession, the racial and economic disparities. Parents who care about education might simply revert to the status quo ante and support unions without investing too much thought in what kinds of reforms could improve educational outcomes. But those who have lost faith in unions, and who care about racial equity in particular, might reconsider their positions on school reform. The roots of modern education accountability standards lie in the Civil Rights Movement, which advocated federal standards and testing to better advocate for students in less advantaged schools.[19] Ohio State's Kogan suggests that parents might now move toward more of a portfolio model of education, seeking options like charters or vouchers. Philanthropists and reformers could take advantage of this opportunity to mobilize greater support for alternatives to traditional education.

The debates about reopening may be binary—are kids in front of computer screens in their homes or are they in classrooms?—and school reopenings will go far to quiet the political divisions between teachers, districts, students, and parents. But these politics will reverberate through an embattled public education system in other ways. They may sow distrust for government and even organized labor. In pushing families toward nonpublic options, they also accelerate a trend evident in so many other areas of public life: the belief that solutions must lie in private, not public, hands.

Notes

1. Kellie Hwang, "Video of Berkeley teachers union chief taking daughter to preschool erupts as flashpoint in reopening battle," San Francisco Chronicle, March 2, 2021 <https://www.sfchronicle.com/bayarea/article/Video-of-Berkeley-teachers-union-chief-taking-15990654.php>.
2. Vladimir Kogan et al., "Who Governs Our Public Schools?" Brown Center Chalkboard (Brookings Institution, Feb. 17, 2021) <https://www.brookings.edu/blog/brown-center-chalkboard/2021/02/17/who-governs-our-public-schools/>.
3. In some districts, teachers also demanded more resources for students, greater support staff, and smaller class sizes.
4. Michael B. Henderson, "Public Support Grows for Higher Teacher Pay and Expanded School Choice," Education Next, August 20, 2019 <https://www.educationnext.org/school-choice-trump-era-results-2019-education-next-poll/>.
5. "Science Brief: Transmission of SARS-CoV-2 in K-12 schools," US Centers for Disease Control and Prevention, March 19, 2021 <https://www.cdc.gov/coronavirus/2019-ncov/science/science-briefs/transmission_k_12_schools.html?CDC_AA_refVal=https%3A%2F%2Fwww.cdc.gov%2Fcoronavirus%2F2019-ncov%2Fmore%2Fscience-and-research%2Ftransmission_k_12_schools.html>; Amelia Nierenberg, "In San Francisco, Closed Public Schools, Open Private Schools," New York Times, Nov. 4, 2020 <https://www.nytimes.com/2020/11/04/us/san-francisco-closed-public-schools-coronavirus.html>.
6. Judith Prieve, "Oakley School Board Gets First of Five New Trustees Following Hot-Mic Scandal," East Bay Times, March 4, 2021 < https://www.eastbaytimes.

com/2021/03/04/oakley-interim-board-appoints-one-trustee-decides-to-do-the-same-with-others/>

7. Helen Lyons, "Some D.C.-Area Private Schools See Increased Interest As Public School Plans Remain Uncertain," Dcist, July 28, 2020 <https://dcist.com/story/20/07/28/dc-region-private-school-enrollment-increase-public-school-uncertain/>; KQED, "Forum: Turbulent Times for San Francisco's School District," March 23, 2021 <https://www.kqed.org/forum/2010101882638/turbulent-times-for-san-franciscos-school-district>; Jill Tucker, "Oakland Schools To Reopen This Month After Striking Tentative Union Deal," San Francisco Chronicle, March 15, 2021 <https://www.sfchronicle.com/education/article/Oakland-strikes-deal-for-schools-to-reopen-16026759.php>

8. Interview with Vladimir Kogan, March 24, 2020.

9. Michael T. Hartney and Leslie K. Finger, "Politics, Markets, and Pandemics: Public Education's Response to COVID-19," EdWorkingPaper: 20-304 (Annenberg Institute at Brown University, October 2020) <https://www.edworkingpapers.com/ai20-304>.

10. Interview with Terry Moe, March 24, 2020.

11. Interview with Michael Hartney, March 24, 2020

12. National Center for Education Statistics, "Back to School Statistics," (US Department of Education, n.d.) <https://nces.ed.gov/fastfacts/display.asp?id=372>.

13. Caitlin Flanagan, "Private Schools Have Become Truly Obscene," The Atlantic, March 11, 2020 <https://www.theatlantic.com/magazine/archive/2021/04/private-schools-are-indefensible/618078/>. Independent schools are a subset of private schools that are independent in their financing and management: They are governed by boards of trustees and funded through tuition and donations.

14. Nikole Hannah-Jones, "Have We Lost Sight of the Promise of Public Schools?" New York Times, Feb. 21, 2017 <https://www.nytimes.com/2017/02/21/magazine/have-we-lost-sight-of-the-promise-of-public-schools.html>.

15. Sasha Abramsky, "West Coast States' Failure to Reopen Schools Is a Disaster," The Nation, Feb. 19, 2021 <https://www.thenation.com/article/society/coronavirus-schools-education-california/>.

16. Edward Isaac-Dovere, "Democrats Are Failing the Schools Test," The Atlantic, March 24, 2021 <https://www.theatlantic.com/politics/archive/2021/03/biden-democrats-school-reopening-politics/618378/>.

17. National Center for Education Statistics, "Charter Schools," (US Department of Education, n.d.) <https://nces.ed.gov/fastfacts/display.asp?id=30>.

18. National Center for Education Statistics, "Racial/Ethnic Enrollment in Public Schools," in The Condition of Education (US Department of Education, last updated May 2020) <https://nces.ed.gov/programs/coe/indicator_cge.asp>.

19. Jesse Hessler Rhodes, "Progressive Policy Making in a Conservative Age? Civil Rights and the Politics of Federal Education Standards, Testing, and Accountability," Perspectives on Politics 9, no. 3 (September 2011): 519-544 <https://www.cambridge.org/core/journals/perspectives-on-politics/article/abs/progressive-policy-making-in-a-conservative-age-civil-rights-and-the-politics-of-federal-education-standards-testing-and-accountability/4075D7756-136F7EBD3611352FFFD63FB>.

> *"Recent data show that the association between education and health has grown dramatically in the last four decades."*

Educated Students Are Healthier Students

Virginia Commonwealth University

In the following viewpoint, Virginia Commonwealth University explores the ways education can impact health. Research suggests that education supports better health for students, both during their schooling years and in their future. In addition, health affects how well students learn. People with educations are safer and healthier, both mentally and physically. Conversely, poor health, family problems, stress, and low socioeconomic status can negatively impact a child's educational performance. All these factors tie together, making education and health intertwined. Virginia Commonwealth University is a public university in Richmond, Virginia.

As you read, consider the following questions:

1. What are the three main connections between health and education, according to the viewpoint?
2. How is stress related to education?
3. How can a neighborhood affect health?

"Why Education Matters to Health: Exploring the Causes," Virginia Commonwealth University, February 13, 2015. Reprinted by permission.

A mericans with more education live longer, healthier lives than those with fewer years of schooling. But why does education matter so much to health? The links are complex—and tied closely to income and to the skills and opportunities that people have to lead healthy lives in their communities.

How are health and education linked? There are three main connections:[1]

- Education can create opportunities for better health
- Poor health can put educational attainment at risk (reverse causality)
- Conditions throughout people's lives—beginning in early childhood—can affect both health and education

The relationship between education and health has existed for generations, despite dramatic improvements in medical care and public health. Recent data show that the association between education and health has grown dramatically in the last four decades. Now more than ever, people who have not graduated high school are more likely to report being in fair or poor health compared to college graduates.[2] Between 1972 and 2004, the gap between these two groups grew from 23 percentage points to 36 percentage points among non-Hispanic whites age 40 to 64. African-Americans experienced a comparable widening in the health gap by education during this time period. The probability of having major chronic conditions also increased more among the least educated.[3] The widening of the gap has occurred across the country.[4]

Research has focused on the number of years of school students complete, largely because there are fewer data available on other aspects of education that are also important. It's not just the diploma: education is important in building knowledge and developing literacy, thinking and problem-solving skills, and character traits. Our community research team noted that early childhood education and youth development are also important to the relationship between education and health.

This issue brief, created with support from the Robert Wood Johnson Foundation, provides an overview of what research shows about the links between education and health alongside the perspectives of residents of a disadvantaged urban community in Richmond, Virginia. These community researchers, members of our partnership, collaborate regularly with the Center on Society and Health's research and policy activities to help us more fully understand the "real life" connections between community life and health outcomes.

1. The Health Benefits of Education

Income and Resources

Better jobs: In today's knowledge economy, an applicant with more education is more likely to be employed and land a job that provides health-promoting benefits such as health insurance, paid leave, and retirement.[5] Conversely, people with less education are more likely to work in high-risk occupations with few benefits.

Higher earnings: Income has a major effect on health and workers with more education tend to earn more money.[2] In 2012, the median wage for college graduates was more than twice that of high school dropouts and more than one and a half times higher than that of high school graduates.[6]

Adults with more education tend to experience less economic hardship, attain greater job prestige and social rank, and enjoy greater access to resources that contribute to better health. A number of studies have suggested that income is among the main reasons for the superior health of people with an advanced education.[1] Weekly earnings rise dramatically for Americans with a college or advanced degree. A higher education has an even greater effect on lifetime earnings, a pattern that is true for men and women, for blacks and whites, and for Hispanics and non-Hispanics. For example, based on 2006-2008 data, the lifetime earnings of a Hispanic male are $870,275 for those with less than a 9th grade education but $2,777,200 for those with a doctoral degree. The corresponding lifetime earnings for a non-Hispanic white male are $1,056,523 and $3,403,123.[7]

Resources for good health: Families with higher incomes can more easily purchase healthy foods, have time to exercise regularly, and pay for health services and transportation. Conversely, the job insecurity, low wages, and lack of assets associated with less education can make individuals and families more vulnerable during hard times—which can lead to poor nutrition, unstable housing, and unmet medical needs.

Economic hardships can harm health and family relationships,[8] as well as making it more difficult to afford household expenses, from utility bills to medical costs. People living in households with higher incomes—who tend to have more education—are more likely to be covered by health insurance. Over time, the insured rate has decreased for Americans without a high school education.

Lower income and lack of adequate insurance coverage are barriers to meeting health care needs. In 2010, more than one in four (27%) adults who lacked a high school education reported being unable to see a doctor due to cost, compared to less than one in five (18%) high school graduates and less than one in 10 (8%) college graduates.[9] Access to care also affects receipt of preventive services and care for chronic diseases. The CDC reports, for example, that about 49% of adults age 50-75 with some high school education were up-to-date with colorectal cancer screening in 2010, compared to 59% of high school graduates and 72% of college graduates.[10]

Social and Psychological Benefits

Reduced stress: People with more education—and thus higher incomes—are often spared the health-harming stresses that accompany prolonged social and economic hardship. Those with less education often have fewer resources (e.g., social support, sense of control over life, and high self-esteem) to buffer the effects of stress.

Life changes, traumas, chronic strain, and discrimination can cause health-harming stress. Economic hardship and other stressors can have a cumulative, negative effect on health over time and may, in turn, make individuals more sensitive to further stressors. Researchers have coined the term "allostatic load" to refer to the effects of chronic exposure to physiological stress responses. Exposure to high allostatic load over time may predispose individuals to diseases such as asthma, cardiovascular disease, gastrointestinal disease, and infections[11] and has been associated with higher death rates among older adults.[12]

Social and psychological skills: Education in school and other learning opportunities outside the classroom build skills and foster traits that are important throughout life and may be important to health, such as conscientiousness, perseverance, a sense of personal control, flexibility, the capacity for negotiation, and the ability to form relationships and establish social networks. These skills can help with a variety of life's challenges—from work to family life—and with managing one's health and navigating the health care system.

Many types of skills can be developed through education, from cognitive skills to problem solving to fostering key personality traits. Education can increase 'learned effectiveness,' including cognitive ability, self-control, and problem solving.[13] Personality traits, otherwise known as 'soft skills,' are associated with success in education and employment and lower mortality rates.[14] One set of these personality traits has been called the 'Big Five': conscientiousness, openness to experience, being extraverted, being agreeable, andemotional stability.[15]

These various forms of human capital are an important way that education affects health. For example, education may strengthen coping skills that reduce the damage of stress. Greater personal control may also lead to healthier behaviors, partly by increasing knowledge. Those with greater perceived personal control are more likely to initiate preventive behaviors.[13]

Social networks: Educated adults tend to have larger social networks—and these connections bring access to financial, psychological, and emotional resources that may help reduce hardship and stress and improve health.

Social networks also enhance access to information and exposure to peers who model acceptable behaviors. The relationship between social support and education may be due, in part, to the social and cognitive skills and greater involvement with civic groups and organizations that come with education.[16, 17] Low social support is associated with higher death rates and poor mental health.[18, 19]

Education is also associated with crime. Among young male high school drop-outs, nearly 1 in 10 was incarcerated on a given day in 2006-2007 versus fewer than 1 of 33 high school graduates.[20] The high incarceration rates in some communities can disrupt social networks and weaken social capital and social control—all of which may impact public health and safety.

Health Behaviors

Knowledge and skills: In addition to being prepared for better jobs, people with more education are more likely to learn about healthy behaviors. Educated patients may be more able to understand their health needs, follow instructions, advocate for themselves and their families, and communicate effectively with health providers.[21]

People with more education are more likely to learn about health and health risks, improving their literacy and comprehension of what can be complex issues critical to their wellbeing. People who are more educated are more receptive to health education campaigns. Education can also lead to more accurate health beliefs and knowledge, and thus to better lifestyle choices, but also to better skills and greater self-advocacy. Education improves skills such as literacy, develops effective habits, and may improve cognitive ability. The skills acquired through education can affect health indirectly (through better jobs and earnings) or directly (through ability to follow health care regimens and manage diseases), and they can affect the ability of patients to navigate the health system, such as knowing how to get reimbursed by a health plan. Thus, more highly educated individuals may be more able to understand health care issues and follow treatment guidelines.[21-23] The quality of doctor-patient communication is also poorer for patients of low socioeconomic status. A review of the effects of health literacy on health found that people with lower health literacy are more likely to use emergency services and be hospitalized and are less likely to use preventive services such as mammography or take medications and interpret labels correctly. Among the elderly, poor health literacy has been linked to poorer health status and higher death rates.[24]

Healthier Neighborhoods

Lower income and fewer resources mean that people with less education are more likely to live in low-income neighborhoods that lack the resources for good health. These neighborhoods are often economically marginalized and segregated and have more risk factors for poor health such as:

- Less access to supermarkets or other sources of healthy food and an oversupply of fast food restaurants and outlets that promote unhealthy foods.[25] Nationwide, access to a store that sells healthier foods is 1.4 less likely in census tracts with fewer college educated adults (less than 27% of the population) than in tracts with a higher proportion of college-educated persons.[26] Food access is important to health because unhealthy eating habits are linked to numerous acute and chronic health problems such as diabetes, hypertension, obesity, heart disease, and stroke as well as higher mortality rates.
- Less green space, such as sidewalks and parks to encourage outdoor physical activity and walking or cycling to work or school.
- Rural and low-income areas, which are more populated by people with less education, often suffer from shortages of primary care physicians and other health care providers and facilities.
- Higher crime rates, exposing residents to greater risk of trauma and deaths from violence and the stress of living

in unsafe neighborhoods. People with less education, particularly males, are more likely to be incarcerated, which carries its own public health risks.

- Fewer high-quality schools, often because public schools are poorly resourced by low property taxes. Low-resourced schools have greater difficulty offering attractive teacher salaries or properly maintaining buildings and supplies.
- Fewer jobs, which can exacerbate the economic hardship and poor health that is common for people with less education.
- Higher levels of toxins, such as air and water pollution, hazardous waste, pesticides, andindustrial chemicals.[27]
- Less effective political influence to advocate for community needs, resulting in a persistent cycle of disadvantage.

2. Poor Health That Affects Education (Reverse Causality)

The relationship between education and health is never a simple one. Poor health not only results from lower educational attainment, it can also cause educational setbacks and interfere with schooling.

For example, children with asthma and other chronic illnesses may experience recurrent absences and difficulty concentrating in class.[28] Disabilities can also affect school performance due to difficulties with vision, hearing, attention, behavior, absenteeism, or cognitive skills.

Health conditions, disabilities, and unhealthy behaviors can all have an effect on educational outcomes. Illness, poor nutrition, substance use and smoking, obesity, sleep disorders, mental health, asthma, poor vision, and inattention/hyperactivity have established links to school performance or attainment.[25, 29, 30] For example, compared to other students, children with attention deficit/ hyperactivity disorder (ADHD) are three times more likely to be held back (retained a grade) and almost three times more likely to drop out of school before graduation.[31] Children who are born with low birth weight also tend to have poorer educational outcomes,[32, 33] and higher risk for special education placements.[34, 35] Although the impact of health on education (reverse causality) is important, many have questioned how large a role it plays.[1]

3. Conditions Throughout the Life Course— Beginning in Early Childhood—That Affect Both Health and Education

A third way that education can be linked to health is by exposure to conditions, beginning in early childhood, which can affect both education and health. Throughout life, conditions at home, socioeconomic status, and other contextual factors can create stress, cause illness, and deprive individuals and families of resources for success in school, the workplace, and healthy living.

Contextual factors throughout one's life can affect education and health. For example, biological characteristics can affect educational success and health outcomes, as can socioeconomic and environmental conditions such as poverty or material deprivation. These influences appear to be particularly acute during early childhood, when children's physical health and academic success can be influenced by biologic risk factors (e.g., low birth weight, chronic health conditions) and socioeconomic status (e.g., parents' education and assets, neighborhood socioeconomic resources, such as day care and schools).[36] School readiness is enhanced by positive early childhood conditions—e.g., fetal wellbeing, social-emotional development, family socioeconomic status, neighborhood socioeconomic status, and early childhood education—but some of these same assets also appear to be vital to the health and development of children and their future risk of adopting unhealthy behaviors and adult diseases.[37-40] Early childhood is a period in which health and educational trajectories are shaped by a nurturing home environment, parental involvement, stimulation, and early childhood education, which can foster the development of social skills, adjustment and emotional regulation as well as learning skills.[41]

A growing body of research suggests that chronic exposure of infants and toddlers to stressors—what experts call "adverse childhood experiences"—can affect brain development and disturb the child's endocrine and immune systems, causing biological changes that increase the risk of heart disease and other conditions later in life. For example:

- The adverse effects of stress on the developing brain and on behavior can affect performance in school and explain setbacks in education. Thus, the correlation between lower educational attainment and illness that is later observed among adults may have as much to do with the seeds of illnessand disability that are planted before children ever reach school age as witheducation itself.
- Children exposed to stress may also be drawn to unhealthy behaviors—such as smoking or unhealthy eating— during adolescence, the age when adult habits are often first established.

Instability in home and community life can have a negative impact on child development and, later in life, such outcomes as economic security and stable housing, which can also affect the physical and mental health of adults. Children exposed to toxic stress, social exclusion and bias, persistent poverty, and trauma experience harmful changes in the architecture of the developing brain that affect cognition, behavioral regulation, and executive function.[42, 43] These disruptions can thereby shape educational, economic, and health outcomes decades and generations later.[44] Dysfunctional coping skills as well as changes in parts of the brain associated with reward and addiction may draw children to unhealthy behaviors (e.g., smoking, alcohol or drug use, unsafe sex, violence) as teenagers.

Focusing on seven categories of adverse childhood experiences (ACEs), researchers in the 1990s reported a "graded relationship" for poor health and chronic disease: the higher the exposure to ACEs as children, the greater the risk as adults of having ischemic heart disease, cancer, stroke, chronic lung disease, and diabetes[45]. Chronic exposure to ACEs is now believed to disrupt children's developing endocrine and immune systems, causing the body to produce stress hormones and proteins that produce chronic inflammation and lead later in life to heart disease and other adult health problems.[46] Chronic stress can also cause epigenetic changes in DNA that "turn on" genes that may cause cancer and other conditions.[47]

Not surprisingly, exposure to ACEs also can stifle success in employment.[38, 48, 49] In one study, the unemployment rate was 13.2% among respondents with 4 or more ACEs, compared to 6.5% for those with no history of ACEs.[50]

People who begin life with adverse childhood experiences can thus end up both with greater illness and with difficulties in school and the workplace, thereby contributing to the link between socioeconomic conditions, education, and health. An important way to improve these outcomes is to address the root causes that expose children to stress in the first place.

| "*The belief that schools are the great equalizer, helping students overcome the inequalities of poverty, is a myth.*"

Education Inequality Has Created an Achievement and Wealth Gap

Kimberly Amadeo

In the following viewpoint Kimberly Amadeo argues that schools in poor areas often have less funding and fewer special programs or extracurricular activities. Students who attend these schools are less prepared for college. In addition, poor families often cannot afford to help pay for their children's higher education. This creates a cycle where poor families remain poor for generations. Because racism contributes to poverty, education inequality contributes to an achievement and earning gap between races. This affects the economy as a whole. Kimberly Amadeo is president of World Money Watch, where she shares her expertise on US and world economies, as well as investing.

As you read, consider the following questions:

1. How does a student's neighborhood affect their educational opportunities?
2. How does education for poorer students help the economy?
3. How do children of college graduates benefit?

"What Is Educational Equity and Why Does It Matter?" by Kimberly Amadeo, The Balance, February 23, 2021. Reprinted by permission.

E quity in education is when every student receives the resources needed to acquire the basic work skills of reading, writing, and simple arithmetic. It measures educational success in society by its outcome, not the resources poured into it.

The ongoing public health and economic crisis has made achieving educational equity even more challenging. In many areas, schools were shut down. This worsened racial disparities, as many low-income families don't have the WiFi connections or computer equipment needed for long-distance learning. A McKinsey study showed that, as a result, students of color were an additional three to five months behind in math, while white students were one to three months behind.[1]

Inequity in education slows economic growth as much as recessions. Students that don't receive the educational resources they need can't perform at their optimal level. They don't earn as much, can't build wealth, and therefore can't afford to send their children to good schools. This continues a cycle of structural inequality that hurts society as a whole.

Defining Educational Equity

Educational equity means the educational system gives each student what he or she needs to perform at an acceptable level.

According to the Organisation for Economic Cooperation and Development (OECD), equity in education has two dimensions that are closely intertwined.

1. Fairness

It means making sure that personal and social circumstances are not obstacles to achieving educational potential. It prohibits discrimination based on gender, ethnic origin, or socioeconomic status.

2. Inclusion

It ensures a basic minimum standard of education for all. For example, everyone should be able to read, write, and do simple arithmetic. If some students need more to get there, they should receive it.[2]

Equity should not be confused with educational equality, which means providing each student the equivalent resources.

Even if every school district gets the same level of funding, it might not be enough to help some students achieve the same level of proficiency. Equality is better than discrimination, but it may not be enough to provide equity.[3]

The Impact of Inequity in Education

Equity in education is necessary for economic mobility. Without it, the economy will suffer from an achievement gap between groups in society. Because some students aren't prepared to achieve their working potential, it creates income inequality, which, in turn, forms a wealth gap.

Parents on the lower-wealth tiers can't afford to send their children to the expensive, quality schools that those on higher tiers can. This contributes to structural inequality, where the institutions themselves contribute to inequality. As a result, inequity in education means that a society loses the income and economic output potential of the lower-income tiers. That slows economic growth for everyone.

Achievement Gap

In the US, inequity in education has created an achievement gap between races. According to research firm Brookings, the average score of Black and Latin students on standardized tests was significantly lower than that of White students.[4]

In an earlier study, McKinsey found that the achievement gap caused by inequity in education has cost the US economy more than all recessions since the 1970s. McKinsey also estimated that, if there had been no achievement gap in the years between 1998 and 2008, US gross domestic product would have been $525 billion higher in 2008. Similarly, if low-income students had the same educational achievement as their wealthier peers over that same period, they would have added $670 billion in GDP.[5]

Education and Income

Inequity in education has increased income inequality in America. Over a lifetime, workers with college degrees earn 84% more than those with only high school diplomas.[6] Meanwhile, those with master's degrees or higher earn 131% more than high school graduates.[7]

Despite this clear economic advantage, fewer than half of Americans age 25-34 have at least a university-level education. Ten other countries, including Korea, Russia, and Canada, rank higher.[8,7]

One reason is that higher education costs so much in the US According to the College Board, one year of a public state school costs $10,560 for in-state students and $27,020 for those from out of state students. Private non-profit education, meanwhile, costs $37,650 a year.[9] The OECD adds the US spends $30,165 per student enrolled in tertiary educational institutions each year, the second highest amount after Luxembourg.[10]

Education and Wealth

A 2018 St. Louis Federal Reserve (FRED) study found there are three ways education creates wealth.

1. Families Headed by College Graduates Earn More

That gives the children a head start in life. They can attend private schools and receive better education themselves.

2. The Upward-Mobility Effect

This occurs when a child is born into a family without a college degree. Once the child earns a diploma, the entire family becomes wealthier. FRED's study found this effect boosted family wealth by 20 percentiles. In families where both the parents and child graduated from college, wealth improved but only by 11 percentiles.

3. The Downward-Mobility Effect
Children whose parents didn't graduate from college fell 10 percentiles in wealth, while those with college-educated parents who didn't graduate from college themselves did worse, falling by 18 percentiles in wealth.[11]

Structural Inequality
Inequity in education has also led to structural inequality. Students in low-income neighborhoods may receive an inferior education compared with students in wealthier areas. Research from Michigan State University (MSU) has found that this school inequality gap accounts for 37% of the reason for their lower math scores.[12] Structural inequality exists where poor children must attend public schools while rich children can afford to attend higher-quality private schools.

"Because of school differences in content exposure for low- and high-income students in this country, the rich are getting richer and the poor are getting poorer," said William Schmidt, an MSU professor of statistics and education, in the study. "The belief that schools are the great equalizer, helping students overcome the inequalities of poverty, is a myth."

How to Achieve Equity in Education
The OECD recommends 10 steps to improve equity in education.[2] Among these are:

Improving the Educational System's Design
The first four steps are laid out to improve the design of educational systems. School districts must make sure each school has the resources it needs for its students. This includes everything from special education to gifted students.

The school system routinely assigns children from an early age to either college-bound or vocational tracks. This often discriminates by gender, race, and income. Instead, the OECD recommends that tracking should be delayed or even eliminated.

Poor-performers should be given extra training so they can "catch up." This includes GED programs. Vocational workers should also receive a college education so they can manage in more high-tech manufacturing.

Providing Personalized Education

The OECD's fifth through seventh steps target the classroom level. Students should receive a personalized education based on their needs.

Instead of failing students, give them intense intervention in specific skill areas. This will increase graduation rates.

Work with parents more to get their support of their child's schoolwork. If this is impossible, then provide after-school programs for those children.

Help immigrants and minority children attend mainstream schools. If needed, give them intense language training.

A University of Michigan study found an 11th solution that was both inexpensive and effective. Researchers sent invitations to high-performing, low-income high school students. It promised scholarships to pay for all costs. More than two-thirds applied to the university compared with 26% in a control group of students who also qualified for financial aid, but did not receive targeted mailings.[13]

Targeting Resources to Those Most in Need

The OECD's steps eight through 10 suggest targeting scarce school funding to those most in need. The United States does the opposite. A US Department of Education study found that 45% of high-poverty schools received less state and local funding than the average for other schools in their district.[14] Similarly, the states that are wealthier have better education scores.[15]

Step eight is to focus on early childhood education. The ninth recommendation says to give grants to children in low-income families to keep them in school. The federal government offers

Pell Grants to low-income students attending college.[16] Step 10 is to set school targets for student skill levels and school dropout rates, and focus resources on those schools with the worst scores.

Endnotes

1. McKinsey & Company. "COVID-10 and Learning Loss - Disparities Grow and Students Need Help. " Accessed Feb. 23, 2021.
2. Organisation for Economic Co-operation and Development (OECD). "Ten Step to Equity in Education." Accessed Feb. 23, 2021.
3. The Education Trust. "Equity and Equality Are Not Equal." Accessed Feb. 23, 2021.
4. Brookings. "Race gaps in SAT scores highlight inequality and hinder upward mobility." Accessed Feb. 23, 2021.
5. McKinsey & Company. "The Economic Cost of the US Education Gap." Accessed Feb. 23, 2021.
6. Georgetown University Center on Education and the Workforce. "The College Payoff." Accessed Feb. 23, 2021.
7. Organisation for Economic Co-operation and Development (OECD). "Education at a Glance 2019." Page 2. Accessed Feb. 23, 2021.
8. Organisation for Economic Co-operation and Development (OECD). "Population with tertiary education." Accessed Feb. 23, 2021.
9. College Board. "Trends in College Pricing: Highlights." Accessed Feb. 23, 2021.
10. Organisation for Economic Co-operation and Development (OECD). "Education at a Glance 2019." Page 2. Accessed Feb. 23, 2021.
11. Federal Reserve Bank of St. Louis. "The Financial Returns from College Across Generations: Large But Unequal." Accessed Feb. 23, 2021.
12. Michigan State University. "Schools Worsen Inequality, Especially in Math Instruction." Accessed Feb. 23, 2021.
13. University of Michigan Ford School. "HAILed it—Tuition-Free Promise Attracts Low-Income Students to U-M." Accessed Feb. 23, 2021.
14. US Department of Education. "Comparability of State and Local Expenditures Among Schools Within Districts: A Report From the Study of School-Level Expenditures," Pages 18-28. Accessed Feb. 23, 2021.
15. Education Next. "America's Mediocre Test Scores." Accessed Feb. 23, 2021.
16. US Department of Education. "Federal Pell Grants Are Usually Awarded Only to Undergraduate Students." https://studentaid.gov/understand-aid/types/grants/pell Accessed Dec. 23, 2020.

Periodical and Internet Sources Bibliography

The following articles have been selected to supplement the diverse views presented in this chapter.

Sandesh Adhikari, "Equity Vs Equality: 20 differences!" Public Health Notes. May 6, 2017. https://www.publichealthnotes.com/equity -vs-equality/

Center for Public Education, "Educational Equity: What Does It Mean? How Do We Know When We Reach It?" 2016. https:// www.nsba.org/-/media/nsba/file/cpe-educational-equity -research-brief-january-2016.

Florida Health, "Health Equality, Health Equity & Health Barriers," http://collier.floridahealth.gov/programs-and-services/wellness -programs/health-equity/_documents/healthequityinfographic .pdf

George Washington University Online Master of Public Health Program, "Equity vs. Equality: What's the Difference?" November 5, 2020. https://onlinepublichealth.gwu.edu/resources/equity-vs -equality/

Global Education Summit, "Education Data Highlights," 2021. https://www.globalpartnership.org/results/education-data -highlights

Ellen Gutoskey, "What's the Difference Between Equity and Equality?" Mental Floss, June 11, 2020. https://www.mentalfloss .com/article/625404/equity-vs-equality-what-is-the-difference

Kurt Hulett, "7 Tips for Achieving Equity in Special Education," rethinkEd, March 06, 2019. https://www.rethinked.com/blog /blog/2019/03/06/7-tips-for-equity-in-special-education/

King University Online, "Equality vs. Equity: A Crucial Difference in Pedagogy," April 20, 2018. https://online.king.edu/news/equality -vs-equity/

Christina A. Samuels, "Are Great Schools Ratings Making Segregation Worse?" Education Week, December 10, 2019. https://www .edweek.org/leadership/are-greatschools-ratings-making -segregation-worse/2019/12

OPPOSING
VIEWPOINTS®
SERIES

CHAPTER 2

How Does Gender Impact Educational Opportunities?

Chapter Preface

If the educational goal is equity—and even basic equality—it is important to address sex, gender expression, and sexual orientation. Girls have faced discrimination in education throughout US history. For much of that history, girls were not expected to enter the workforce and few careers were open to women. Girls' education focused on homemaking skills, along with basic reading and writing. In the 1920s, women started entering the workforce in larger numbers, but they were still directed to fields seen as more traditionally feminine. That continued through the 1980s and to some extent still exists today.

Women face many barriers in the workplace. They are underrepresented in some fields, especially those involving science, math, and technology. They are often paid less than male coworkers doing similar jobs. Social attitudes about gender continue to hold women back in many careers.

These biases start early in the educational system. For example, studies have found that teachers rate boys as more mathematically able than girls even when the two performed equally well. Teachers subconsciously underrate their girl students in math, leading to an achievement gap by third grade. It is hard to overcome such early training in what girls and boys can and should do.

The situation is much worse in low-income countries. There, girls may not even complete primary education. They marry younger and have more children, which has a lifelong effect on their health and income. Studies prove that educating girls benefits the girls as individuals and the community as well. International organizations are promoting change, but societies often change slowly if at all.

Boys are not immune from educational challenges. Studies suggest that girls are ready for school earlier than boys are. This readiness is based on maturity, independence, and organizational skills, along with emotional factors. Boys may take longer to develop in certain areas, which can lead to teachers seeing those boys as poor learners. Young boys may struggle in school when classrooms and curricula are not designed for their interests and activity levels. When boys fail early in school, they may develop a dislike of school that interferes with their education for years.

LGB students face additional challenges, such as bullying. Few schools actively address these problems to protect LGB students. When children are unhappy and concerned for their safety, it is hard to learn.

Achieving equity in education means giving every child the support they need. The viewpoints in this chapter explore the issues surrounding sex and gender in education.

> "The obstacles that women face are largely societal and cultural. They act against women from the time they enter kindergarten—instilling in very young girls a belief they are less innately talented than their male peers—and persist into their work lives."

Education and Educators Discriminate Against Girls

Joseph Cimpian

In the following viewpoint Joseph Cimpian argues that the education system undervalues girls and does not support them to their full potential. He notes that a gap in math test scores between Black and white students could be because of the schools the students attend. However, a gap in math test scores also exists between male and female students who attend the same schools. Students start out equal in kindergarten, but the gap grows quickly in elementary school. The author suggests that this gap is due to teacher biases. Teachers tend to assume boys have more mathematical ability. This kind of discrimination affects girls throughout their schooling, into college, and even during their careers. Joseph Cimpian is an associate professor of economics and education policy at NYU Steinhardt.

"How Our Education System Undermines Gender Equity," by Joseph Cimpian, The Brookings Institution, April 23, 2018. Reprinted by permission.

As you read, consider the following questions:

1. How do teacher assumptions about the abilities of girls versus boys affect students?
2. Are girls more or less likely to enter a field that is known for discrimination against women?
3. Why does the author say that changing policy is not enough to change the outcomes of discrimination against girls?

There are well-documented achievement and opportunity gaps by income and race/ethnicity. K-12 accountability policies often have a stated goal of reducing or eliminating those gaps, though with questionable effectiveness. Those same accountability policies require reporting academic proficiency by gender, but there are no explicit goals of reducing gender gaps and no "hard accountability" sanctions tied to gender-subgroup performance. We could ask, "Should gender be included more strongly in accountability policies?"

In this post, I'll explain why I don't think accountability policy interventions would produce real gender equity in the current system—a system that largely relies on existing state standardized tests of math and English language arts to gauge equity. I'll argue that although much of the recent research on gender equity from kindergarten through postgraduate education uses math or STEM parity as a measure of equity, the overall picture related to gender equity is of an education system that devalues young women's contributions and underestimates young women's intellectual abilities more broadly.

In a sense, math and STEM outcomes simply afford insights into a deeper, more systemic problem. In order to improve access and equity across gender lines from kindergarten through the workforce, we need considerably more social-questioning and self-assessment of biases about women's abilities.

As Soon as Girls Enter School, They Are Underestimated

For over a decade now, I have studied gender achievement with my colleague Sarah Lubienski, a professor of math education at Indiana University-Bloomington. In a series of studies using data from both the 1998-99 and 2010-11 kindergarten cohorts of the nationally representative Early Childhood Longitudinal Study, we found that no average gender gap in math test scores existed when boys and girls entered kindergarten, but a gap of nearly 0.25 standard deviations developed in favor of the boys by around second or third grade.

For comparison purposes, the growth of the black-white math test score gap was virtually identical to the growth in the gender gap. Unlike levels and growth in race-based gaps, though, which have been largely attributed to a combination of differences in the schools attended by black and white students and to socio-economic differences, boys and girls for the most part attend the same schools and come from families of similar socio-economic status. This suggests that something may be occurring within schools that contributes to an advantage for boys in math.

Exploring deeper, we found that the beliefs that teachers have about student ability might contribute significantly to the gap. When faced with a boy and a girl of the same race and socio-economic status who performed equally well on math tests and whom the teacher rated equally well in behaving and engaging with school, the teacher rated the boy as more mathematically able—an alarming pattern that replicated in a separate data set collected over a decade later.

Another way of thinking of this is that in order for a girl to be rated as mathematically capable as her male classmate, she not only needed to perform as well as him on a psychometrically rigorous external test, but also be seen as working harder than him. Subsequent matching and instrumental variables analyses suggested that teachers' underrating of girls from kindergarten through third grade accounts for about half of the gender achievement gap growth in math. In other words, if teachers didn't think their female students were less capable, the gender gap in math might be substantially smaller.

An interaction that Sarah and I had with a teacher drove home the importance and real-world relevance of these results. About five years ago, while Sarah and I were faculty at the University of Illinois, we gathered a small group of elementary teachers together to help us think through these findings and how we could intervene on the notion that girls were innately less capable than boys. One of the teachers pulled a stack of papers out of her tote bag, and spreading them on the conference table, said, "Now, I don't even understand why you're looking at girls' math achievement. These are my students' standardized test scores, and there are absolutely no gender differences. See, the girls can do just as well as the boys if they work hard enough." Then, without anyone reacting, it was as if a light bulb went on. She gasped and continued, "Oh my gosh, I just did exactly what you said teachers are doing," which is attributing girls' success in math to hard work while attributing boys' success to innate ability. She concluded, "I see now why you're studying this."

Although this teacher did ultimately recognize her gender-based attribution, there are (at least) three important points worth noting. First, her default assumption was that girls needed to work harder in order to achieve comparably to boys in math, and this reflects an all-too-common pattern among elementary school teachers, across at least the past couple decades and in other cultural contexts. Second, it is not obvious how to get teachers to change that default assumption. Third, the evidence that she brought to the table was state standardized test scores, and these types of tests can reveal different (often null or smaller) gender achievement gaps than other measures.

On this last point, state standardized tests consistently show small or no differences between boys and girls in math achievement, which contrasts with somewhat larger gaps on NAEP and PISA, as well as with gaps at the top of the distribution on the ECLS,

SAT Mathematics assessment, and the American Mathematics Competition. The reasons for these discrepancies are not entirely clear, but what is clear is that there is no reason to expect that "hardening" the role of gender in accountability policies that use existing state tests and current benchmarks will change the current state of gender gaps. Policymakers might consider implementing

Girls' Education Is a Lifeline to Development

Among children not attending school there are twice as many girls as boys, and among illiterate adults there are twice as many women as men.

What would it take to improve girls' access to education? Experience in scores of countries shows the importance, among other things, of:

- Parental and community involvement—Families and communities must be important partners with schools in developing curriculum and managing children's education.
- Low-cost and flexible timetables—Basic education should be free or cost very little. Where possible, there should be stipends and scholarships to compensate families for the loss of girls' household labour. Also, school hours should be flexible so children can help at home and still attend classes.
- Schools close to home, with women teachers—Many parents worry about girls travelling long distances on their own. Many parents also prefer to have daughters taught by women.
- Preparation for school—Girls do best when they receive early childhood care, which enhances their self-esteem and prepares them for school.
- Relevant curricula—Learning materials should be relevant to the girl's background and be in the local language. They should also avoid reproducing gender stereotypes.

"Girls' Education: A Lifeline to Development," UNICEF.

test measures similar to those where gaps have been noted and placing more emphasis on gains throughout the achievement distribution. However, I doubt that a more nuanced policy for assessing math gains would address the underlying problem of the year-after-year underestimation of girls' abilities and various signals and beliefs that buttress boys' confidence and devalue girls, all of which cumulatively contributes to any measured gaps.

More Obstacles Await Women in Higher Education and Beyond

Looking beyond K-12 education, there is mounting evidence at the college and postgraduate levels that cultural differences between academic disciplines may be driving women away from STEM fields, as well as away from some non-STEM fields (e.g., criminal justice, philosophy, and economics). In fact, although research and policy discussions often dichotomize academic fields and occupations as "STEM" and "non-STEM," the emerging research on gender discrimination in higher education finds that the factors that drive women away from some fields cut across the STEM/non-STEM divide. Thus, while gender representation disparities between STEM and non-STEM fields may help draw attention to gender representation more broadly, reifying the STEM/non-STEM distinction and focusing on math may be counterproductive to understanding the underlying reasons for gender representation gaps across academic disciplines.

In a recent study, my colleagues and I examined how perceptions on college majors relate to who is entering those majors. We found that the dominant factor predicting the gender of college-major entrants is the degree of perceived discrimination against women. To reach this conclusion, we used two sources of data. First, we created and administered surveys to gather perceptions on how much math is required for a major, how much science is required, how creative a field is, how lucrative careers are in a field, how helpful the field is to society, and how difficult it is for a woman to succeed in the field. After creating factor scales on each of the six dimensions for each major, we mapped those ratings onto the second data source, the Education Longitudinal Study, which contains several prior achievement, demographic, and attitudinal measures on which we matched young men and women attending four-year colleges.

Among this nationally representative sample, we found that the degree to which a field was perceived to be math- or science-intensive had very little relation to student gender. However, fields that were perceived to discriminate against women were strongly predictive of the gender of the students in the field, whether or not we accounted for the other five traits of the college majors. In short, women are less likely to enter fields where they expect to encounter discrimination.

And what happens if a woman perseveres in obtaining a college degree in a field where she encounters discrimination and underestimation and wants to pursue a postgraduate degree in that field, and maybe eventually work in academia? The literature suggests additional obstacles await her. These obstacles may take the form of those in the field thinking she's not brilliant like her male peers in graduate school, having her looks discussed on online job boards when she's job-hunting, performing more service work if she becomes university faculty, and getting less credit for co-authored publications in some disciplines when she goes up for tenure.

Each of the examples here and throughout this post reflects a similar problem—education systems (and society) unjustifiably and systematically view women as less intellectually capable.

Societal Changes Are Necessary

My argument that policy probably isn't the solution is not intended to undercut the importance of affirmative action and grievance policies that have helped many individuals take appropriate legal recourse. Rather, I am arguing that those policies are certainly not enough, and that the typical K-12 policy mechanisms will likely have no real effect in improving equity for girls.

The obstacles that women face are largely societal and cultural. They act against women from the time they enter kindergarten—instilling in very young girls a belief they are less innately talented than their male peers—and persist into their work lives. Educational institutions—with undoubtedly many well-intentioned educators—are themselves complicit in reinforcing the hurdles. In order to dismantle these barriers, we likely need educators at all levels of education to examine their own biases and stereotypes.

> *"If women have relatively more education compared to their partners, they may be more likely to choose to have, and achieve, fewer children, and hence be at lower risk of dying in childbirth."*

Educating Girls Saves Lives

Sonia R. Bhalotra and Damian Clarke

In the following viewpoint Sonia R. Bhalotra and Damian Clarke address the problem of women who die in childbirth. A higher percentage of women die in childbirth in the poorest and least developed countries. This is partly due to health availability, but the authors argue that education is an important part of health. Girls who receive even a few years of schooling are less likely to die in childbirth. They have more knowledge and are more likely to understand and address health concerns. In addition, educated girls can make better choices in who they marry and often choose to have fewer children. Therefore, this author argues that worldwide, educating girls should be a priority for both social justice and health reasons. Sonia Bhalotra is a professor of economics at the University of Essex. Damian Clarke is an associate professor of economics at the University of Santiago de Chile.

"Does Women's Education Reduce Rates of Death in Childbirth?," by Sonia R. Bhalotra and Damian Clarke, November 2016, WIDERAngle. This content is reproduced here with full acknowledgement of the publisher UNU-WIDER, Helsinki. Reprinted by permission.

As you read, consider the following questions:

1. How can the number of women who die in childbirth be reduced?
2. What is the relationship between the years of education among women and rates of maternal death in childbirth?
3. Does offering more education for men reduce childbirth deaths for women?

Every single day, approximately 830 women die from causes related to childbirth. Despite considerable advances in maternal health over the last three decades (Hogan et al. 2010) as well as worldwide commitment to reducing maternal deaths, sufficient reductions have not been achieved. These deaths are overwhelmingly preventable provided that timely access to appropriate obstetric care and contraceptives are available (Ronsmans and Graham 2006; Ahmed et al. 2012).

The newly defined Sustainable Development Goals (SDGs) aim to address this failure and reduce the rate of maternal death to 70 per 100,000 live births by 2030, from 210 per 100,000 today. Meeting this goal requires advances in the poorest and least developed countries, which have by far the highest rates of maternal mortality world-wide. Our research suggests that—in addition to addressing health infrastructure, accessibility in remote regions, and work with marginalized groups—boosting girls' education may be an important policy lever in curtailing the 830 deaths occurring every day.

Why Education Might Matter

Policy documents on maternal mortality seldom indicate education as a factor and the academic literature has very little to say about the relationship between maternal mortality and education. This said, there is a lively literature in economics that documents a positive correlation between education and other indicators of health.

The immediate causes of maternal mortality are pregnancy-related complications such as pre-eclampsia, bleeding, infections and unsafe abortion. To the extent that educated women are more likely to adopt simple and low-cost practices to maintain hygiene, are more able to react to symptoms such as bleeding or high blood pressure, more likely to access the information on abortion and place of abortion, and more willing to accept treatment and trained birth attendants, education may plausibly cause declines in maternal mortality.

Findings Show Education Reduces Maternal Mortality at Global Level

World-wide, rates of schooling and literacy have increased substantially over the past century. Similarly, and particularly since 2000, rates of maternal deaths in childbirth have fallen by an impressive amount. Generally speaking, as the years of education among women rise, rates of maternal death in childbirth fall. Nevertheless, these correlations may represent many external factors, including changing rates of national investment in health and education, economic growth, the strengthening of national institutions or a demographic transition.

The results of our study suggest, first, that even when controlling for alternative explanations, the level of female education in a country has considerable effects on rates of maternal death. Interestingly, when estimating the conditional effect of women's education and men's education together, it is increases in women's education in a country that reduce rates of maternal death, and not simultaneous increases in men's education. This suggests that rather than simply reflecting a correlation between secular increases in education and declines in maternal mortality, the effect of women-specific education drives reductions in maternal mortality. Similarly, efforts to raise education alone will not lead to reductions in rates of maternal death unless the education of girls in particular is targeted.

Second, our results suggest that not all increases in women's education bring about the same effects. Attaining basic health knowledge at low levels of education may have important effects on an individual's likelihood of dying in child birth. Moving an additional one per cent of women into primary education (from no education) would reduce rates of maternal death by between 5-8 deaths per 100,000 live births, which is four per cent of the mean value of maternal death during the period under study. The additional effect of moving women into secondary education is significant, but lower in magnitude, while the effect of moving women into tertiary education is not significantly different to zero.

All in all, the study shows through estimated effects that comparable changes—that is, one standard deviation movement in each variable—in women's primary education and GDP per capita would have an impact of similar magnitude on rates of maternal death. This is important, given that recent WHO fact sheets on maternal mortality highlight differences in maternal mortality ratios by income, but not education level.

Effects of Education Seen Clearly in Countries with Educational Reforms

The findings hold true when we look specifically at countries that have sharply expanded educational attainment. For example, in the case of Nigeria (a Universal Primary Education reform) and Zimbabwe (a lower secondary school reform), cohorts of women affected by the education expansions had significantly lower levels of maternal mortality later in life as compared to those who were otherwise similar, but not impacted by the educational reforms. This was most pronounced when the reform moved women from no schooling to primary schooling.

Education as Empowerment

There are a number of reasons by which women's education may reduce rates of maternal death, with recent work by Ashraf et al. (2012, 2014) pointing to empowerment (or women's bargaining power) as a potentially relevant mechanism. If women have relatively more education compared to their partners, they may be more likely to choose to have, and achieve, fewer children, and hence be at lower risk of dying in childbirth.

In our study, we found that, as suggested by Ashraf and colleagues, education is particularly effective when it allows women to "catch up" with men. When women become more educated relative to men, they report being less likely to be involved in partnerships with men who want more children than they do, which in turn has considerable follow-on effects to rates of maternal death.

A Call to Action: Boosting Girls' Education to Meet Broader Development Goals

Maternal mortality rates need to be reduced by two-thirds over the next 15 years to meet the Sustainable Development Goals. Our research, discussed above, shows that a focus on girl's education may be one means of meeting this objective. Quality education for all is also an important human development goal in its own right. Indeed, its inclusion as a Sustainable Development Goal itself means that crosscutting relationships between education and other indicators make investments in quality schooling and learning a particularly important and cost-effective global goal.

> *"Early childhood programs, in general, provide a goodness-of-fit between all aspects of the program and the needs of girls. Almost all staff in programs for young children are women."*

School Is Not Designed for Boys

Francis Wardle

In the following viewpoint Francis Wardle argues that girls often do better in school, especially at an early age, while boys more often struggle with behavioral problems. Their behavior may be natural to young boys, but schools are not usually designed to accept that behavior. When boys lag in their development, they may be identified as troubled learners, when in reality they simply need more time. Teachers may scold and punish boys for their behavior, leading to shame and a dislike of school. This can lead to academic problems in later schooling, including a risk of dropping out. Francis Wardle has a PhD in child development and early education from the University of Kansas. He has taught preschool, kindergarten, and grades 1-4.

As you read, consider the following questions:

1. Why do girls often do better than boys in school?
2. How can school be changed to encourage boys' success?
3. How can classrooms be "boy-friendly"?

"The Challenge of Boys in Early Childhood Education," by Francis Wardle, Community Playthings, www.communityplaythings.com, August 9, 2016. Reprinted by permission.

I have a wonderful photo on my screen saver of my kindergarten class. They are playing in the Pennsylvania woods next to a large pond. The girls are playing together around a picnic table under a beautiful maple tree; the boys are all down by the lake. Actually, most of the boys are sitting on large boulders in the lake! And—most curiously—each boy has a stick in his hand. Some are fishing with them; others are using them to collect leaves, twigs, and other floating debris from the water.

While my kindergarten class does most things together, including growing a flower garden, caring for a group of laying hens, and playing outdoor games, the separation in this picture is very distinct. Further, while the girls are playing a distance from the water, the boys are actually in it, pushing safety and taking risks (and yes, I am very carefully supervising!).

Boys like to take risks. They love rough-and-tumble play, make lots of noise, and enjoy messing around with water, sticks, mud, and sand. They are spontaneous, impulsive, fun-loving, and mistake prone! But many young boys struggle in organized early childhood programs.

The Facts

- Boys represent 61 percent of kindergarteners held back from moving into first grade.
- While boys represent 54 percent of the preschool population, they represent 79 percent of preschool children suspended once, and 82 percent of preschool children suspended multiple times.
- Boys are almost 5 times more likely to be expelled from preschool than girls.
- Boys are 2 to 4 times more likely to be identified with a learning disability (the largest of the federal special education categories) than girls.*
- ADHD is diagnosed 3 to 4 times more often in male compared to female students.*

Goodness of Fit

The work of Thomas and Chess (1977) introduced the concept of "goodness-of-fit." This is an idea which shows that, for optimal development, a match must be created between a child's temperament and their social environment.

This match is a pattern of social interactions between the child and his caregivers (Berger, 2003). Thus parents, child care providers, and teachers need to be in tune with each child's idiosyncratic temperament. This goodness-of-fit is critical for the child's future emotional, cognitive, physical, and social development.

It is now clear that the idea of goodness-of-fit goes well beyond temperament, and must include a close match between all of the young child's developmental needs and their social and physical environments. And it is clear that many programs do not provide this goodness-of-fit for our young boys.

Reasons Many Boys Struggle in Early Childhood Programs

There are a number of reasons many young boys struggle in early childhood programs. Some of these include:

In general, the development of boys' brains and overall nervous systems is delayed compared to girls (Berk, 2002; Leaper, Anderson & Sanders, 1998). And, since the brain controls cognitive development, attention, and emotional regulation (the ability to control one's own behavior), this delay directly impacts attention span, activity levels, and overall academic development. Boys' impulsivity and poor self-regulation are directly tied to their immature brain development.

The curriculum and activities in most early childhood programs focus on literacy activities, the arts (often more crafts), and social-dramatic play, along with behaviors deemed necessary to achieve these activities. It is well known that young girls' verbal skills surpass those of young boys (Owens, 2012). Boys prefer wild, aggressive, full-body activities, constructive play, hands-on learning with concrete materials, and lots of movement. They also seem to love to make a mess!

The current push-down of K-12 curricula expectations, along with unrealistic behavior expectations, has resulted in more and more boys struggling to meet academic standards. As a result, a disproportionate number of boys are being expelled, suspended, or placed in special education.

Because of the focus on meeting academic, school-related standards, "school readiness" early childhood programs focus their budgets and teacher training on literacy programs, technology, countless assessments, and classroom management, as opposed to well-equipped playgrounds, indoor gross motor rooms, in-depth projects, and a variety of field trips.

Early childhood programs, in general, provide a goodness-of-fit between all aspects of the program (curriculum, activities, involvement of teachers) and the needs of girls. Almost all staff in programs for young children are women.

We have created a fix the child syndrome (as opposed to change the program). Early intervention approaches, multiple assessments, and a focus on what is considered normal development, have led to a need to identify and label children who struggle in our programs. This in turn has led both to a belief by these children that they cannot succeed, and that the program selects winners and losers (Kohn, 1993).

Solutions

Some of the suggested solutions can be met in the ways we interact with children, choose activities, teach our children, structure our classrooms, and schedule the day. But others will require systematic changes in the entire early childhood field—at least in the United States.

The first, and most important, change to be made is to fully recognize that, in some fundamental ways, young boys and young girls are different, which means they must be treated differently (goodness-of-fit). This does not mean inequality; as every parent knows, treating each of their children exactly the same is a formula for disaster! We must not confuse sameness with equality. Other suggestions include:

Radically reevaluate our focus on outcome standards. Standards for quality program performance are fine; outcome standards, especially academic and behavioral standards that are not developmentally appropriate for all children, are a huge problem, especially for many boys. We need to go back to a true understanding of developmentally appropriate practice (Wardle, 1999); we also need to take lessons from countries like Finland, where quality early childhood programs do not sacrifice developmentally appropriate practice.

Shift the overall focus of early childhood curricula and activities to hands-on experiences, whole body physical activities (inside and outside), whole-child learning, and developmentally appropriate science and mechanical projects; return play to the center of the curriculum, and use flexible daily schedules with large blocks of time. A variety of in-depth projects should also be incorporated into the curriculum.

Embrace the natural variability of the development of young children. There is a tendency to view average developmental trends as milestones, which of course penalizes children who are naturally behind in one or more domains. Further, a vast variety of approaches need to be tried before referring a child to be screened for possible special needs. These approaches include working closely with parents, changing the curriculum, differentiating activities, using different learning styles to perform a task or activity, and so on.

Never withhold activities a child enjoys doing, and is competent in performing, as an incentive to complete an activity or task a child struggles with (the Premack principle). All children—but especially those who struggle, both academically and behaviorally—need lots of opportunities to be successful, even if it's simply playing on the playground or painting a fantastic picture (Erikson, 1963).

Increase the number of men in early childhood programs. This is one of those long-term systemic challenges requiring: 1) increasing the number of fathers, grandfathers, older brothers, and community volunteers in our programs, and 2) a paradigm shift both in terms of our culture's view of men (nurturing, supportive, emotional), and society's view of men's ability to care for young children.

Make classrooms more boy-friendly. Provide a woodwork center; redo the dramatic play area (drop the term housekeeping); carefully select books on subjects of interest to boys; and make sure there is lots of time every day for a variety of outdoor activities, including exploring nature. The dramatic play area needs to include props such as hard hats, brief cases, tools, fire fighter hoses, police uniforms, sports hats and uniforms, etc. Books need to include heroes, monsters, construction, vehicles, huge earth-moving machinery, messy activities, and so on.

Summary

Many boys struggle in our early childhood programs. This is evident by the disproportionate number of young boys who are suspended, expelled, and/or placed into special education programs. This is no accident. To address these discrepancies, a variety of approaches need to be taken, from radically changing some fundamental practices of the field, to adjusting the curriculum, activities, environments, and teacher-child interactions.

*These statistics are for children 6 years and older, because we don't have statistics for children under age six. One can only assume these figures would be even higher for young boys! (Cortiella, 2011; Gilliam, 2005; Lerner & Johns, 2012; US Centers for Disease Control and Prevention, 2013; US Department of Education, Office of Civil Rights, 2016).

> "Educators still have a tremendous amount of worry around LGBTQ inclusion—they fear parent or community pushback, and are uncertain if they'd be supported by school or district leadership if they took action."

LGBTQ+ Students Need Protection

Emelina Minero

In the following viewpoint Emelina Minero explores challenges LGBTQ+ students may have in school. Bullying, from cyber harassment to physical violence, is especially high against LGBTQ+ students. This can lead to a variety of serious problems, from absenteeism to suicide attempts. However, teachers and administrators struggle to address problems and support LGBTQ+ students. While most teachers want to make school safe for these students, few schools provide training in how to do so. In addition, teachers often fear a backlash from parents or the community if they actively support LGBTQ+ students. Emelina Minero is an assistant editor at Edutopia, a foundation dedicated to improving K-12 education.

As you read, consider the following questions:

1. How many states had legislation in place for protecting LGBTQ+ students, at the time of this writing?
2. Why do many teachers feel uncertain of how to help LGBTQ+ students?
3. How can schools and individual teachers help support and protect LGBTQ+ students?

P inning Roddy Biggs against a locker, a student whaled on him, giving him a black eye, fracturing his eye socket, and bruising his ribs. It wasn't a lone incident for Biggs, who came out as gay to his Tennessee high school when he was a freshman.

"I didn't really do the best in school because of it," recalls Biggs, now 23, who says homophobic slurs, death threats, and shoves were commonplace. "I had depression and panic attacks and all that stuff along the way."

Biggs can still remember the teachers who ignored the bullying or simply said, "That's not cool," and walked away. But there were also the educators who tried to help, like the science teacher who took him to the principal's office after he was beaten and sat with him for more than an hour during class time. Oftentimes, though, the best efforts of teachers were stymied by district or state regulations that stopped them from doing much more.

"Most of the educators wanted to help, but did not know how or were limited in what they could do," says Biggs, referring to Tennessee's lack of legislation preventing the bullying of lesbian, gay, bisexual, transgender, and queer or questioning (LGBTQ) students. Tennessee is one of 32 states that do not have such protections in place.

From cyberharassment to physical violence, bullying is a serious problem for many schools, but bullying LGBTQ students in particular is more likely to be ignored or mishandled by staff, according to recent research.

The researchers surveyed nearly 2,500 teachers and students across the country and found that teachers were less comfortable intervening with bullying due to sexual orientation and gender identity than with bullying based on race, ability, and religion. And while 83 percent of educators felt that they should provide a safe environment for their LGBTQ students—by displaying visible symbols of support or disciplining students for using homophobic language, for example—only half had taken action to do so, according to the Gay, Lesbian and Straight Education Network (GLSEN), an organization that helps K–12 schools create safe environments for LGBTQ students.

This lack of support for LGBTQ students stems from a variety of causes.

Some teachers reported feeling uncomfortable talking to their students about sexuality due to their beliefs or perceptions about what's appropriate—often conflating sexual orientation with sex—while others felt pressure from administrators or parents to keep tight-lipped. And a lack of professional development on how to address LGBTQ issues and bullying has left teachers ill-equipped to establish LGBTQ-inclusive cultures or to identify anti-LGBTQ behaviors and harassment. Meanwhile, the emergence of highly politicized issues like allowing transgender students to use bathrooms aligned with their identity has raised the LGBTQ profile nationally, but made constructive dialogue harder.

The Need for Training

For Loretta Farrell Khayam, a high school math teacher in Northern Virginia, the hesitation to support LGBTQ students reflects a simple lack of training.

"We've had no guidance from administration on how to handle students transitioning," said Khayam, who wants to help a transgender student at her school. "I'm not a young, hip teacher. I don't know what to say or do. It would be nice to hear from our administration—both school and district level—what we as a school and a school system will do to support these students."

While there has been an increased interest in training educators on topics like inherent bias and equity and inclusion, these trainings often do not include LGBTQ issues because most school systems aren't requesting it, according to educators and advocacy groups. And when teachers have asked for training, some report that they've faced reluctance from administrators who said they need to focus on other priorities.

Melissa Joy Bollow Tempel said she encountered pushback when she wanted to start including professional development on gender identity in the training she provided as a culturally responsive teacher-leader in the Milwaukee Public Schools district. Bollow Tempel had to go outside the district to receive training herself, and her offers to share what she had learned were repeatedly resisted.

Even within the 18 states with anti-bullying laws aimed at protecting both sexual orientation and gender identity, and within "blue bubbles" like California, both discomfort and neglect are common, according to Vincent Pompei, director of the Youth Well-Being Project at the Human Rights Campaign, the largest LGBTQ civil rights organization in the US Pompei noted that attendees at a recent training in Southern California couldn't differentiate sexual orientation from gender identity.

"Educators still have a tremendous amount of worry around LGBTQ inclusion—they fear parent or community pushback, and are uncertain if they'd be supported by school or district leadership if they took action," Pompei said. "We say students need to see visible signs of a safe space, but educators also need to know that their administration supports them and will have their back if a parent or community member with anti-LGBTQ views complains."

Avoidable Struggles

When LGBTQ students feel the lack of staff support at school, the impact can be substantial.

Lesbian, gay, and bisexual students are two to three times as likely to be bullied as non-LGBTQ peers, and they're more likely to miss school and almost five times as likely to attempt suicide—the number is even higher for transgender people—according to a major survey of 15,600 high school students by the Centers for Disease Control and Prevention. Another study found that bullied lesbian, gay, and bisexual students reported higher levels of substance abuse and risky behaviors than heterosexual students who were bullied.

"My middle school didn't have any procedures, and my teachers didn't know what to do," reflects Miles Sanchez, a ninth-grade bisexual and transgender student in Colorado. Sanchez says he repeatedly went to administrators to ask them to establish policies to protect LGBTQ students from bullying. "I feel like a lot of my struggles could have been avoided if educators were trained in dealing with bullying for all types of students," he said.

The problem is not restricted to students.

Teachers like Hanan Huneidi, a 7th- through 12-grade teacher for at-risk students in the Bay Area, California, says she feels that if she includes LGBTQ content in her lessons, staff and students assume she's trying to push a particular agenda because she's gay. Huneidi says she has at times avoided the topic because she doesn't always want to "automatically be the representative of all gay things."

Last year, a frustrated Huneidi told colleagues they needed to "carry the torch too" in disciplining students for using homophobic hate language, which is against school rules.

Creating a Safe Space

To address the need for more awareness, organizations like Gender Spectrum and History UnErased are providing professional development and support for K–12 classrooms. Resources provided by these organizations include lesson plans, workshops, and guides.

And some districts, like the Madison Metropolitan School District in Madison, Wisconsin, are embedding professional development directly into their schools. The district has a staff social worker in charge of LGBTQ-specific staff training and family support, and last year the district adopted the LGBTQ professional development program Welcoming Schools.

As part of the program, district staff members—including school psychologists, social workers, and teachers—received training so they can coach their colleagues on topics like embracing family diversity and preventing bias-based bullying. The district also hosts parent and student panels to share LGBTQ students' experiences with staff, and community events, like readings of children's books with LGBTQ characters.

But according to LGBTQ advocates, it doesn't take a top-down approach to make a difference in students' lives—help can come from a single educator.

Sometimes it's as simple as putting up safe space signs, or a sign that says a classroom or school is welcoming of all identities; reprimanding a student who uses the phrase "that's so gay"; or reading a book with an LGBTQ protagonist. Small changes from one person can often lead to bigger ones from more.

Dan Ryder, a teacher at Mount Blue High School in Farmington, Maine, said he's personally seen change happen slowly over the nearly two decades that he's worked at his school. He remembers the days of "don't ask, don't tell" and the widespread use of homophobic slurs. Now, he says, students in the school's tech program are making signs to affix to new gender-neutral bathrooms of their own accord.

"I'm doing my best to show them that even though I may be a straight, cis, married white male, we are all fairly complex beings that change over time and have experiences that may unite us more than we realize," he says of his own efforts to help students. "Often we just need someone to say, 'Hey, you are who you are. I get it. It's OK by me. And I want to be helpful to you in whatever way that means for you.'"

Periodical and Internet Sources Bibliography

The following articles have been selected to supplement the diverse views presented in this chapter.

Shannon Andrus, Charlotte E. Jacobs, and Peter Kuriloff, "Miles to go: The continuing quest for gender equity in the classroom," September 24, 2018. Kaplan. https://kappanonline.org/andrus -jacobs-kuriloff-gender-equity-classroom/

Global Poverty Project, "Education Is the Most Important Investment to Make to End Poverty," https://www.globalcitizen.org/en /content/the-value-of-education/

Erin Hinrichs, "A Q&A with Kelly Holstine: on advancing educational equity for LGBTQ students," MinnPost, October 22, 2019. https://www.minnpost.com/education/2019/10/a-qa -with-kelly-holstine-on-advancing-educational-equity-for-lgbtq -students/

International Commission on Financing Global Education, "The Learning Generation," https://report.educationcommission.org /report/

Grainne Kent, "Gender differences in cognitive development and school readiness," Children's Research Network, December 2018. https://www.childrensresearchnetwork.org/knowledge/resources /gender-differences-in-cognitive-development-and-school -readiness

Aurelio M. Montemayor and Michelle Martínez Vega, "Equity and Justice for LGBTQ Students—Teacher Responsibilities," IDRA, February 2018. https://www.idra.org/resource-center/equity -justice-lgbtq-students-teacher-responsibilities/

Elina Pradhan, Elina M Suzuki, Sebastián Martínez, Marco Schäferhoff, and Dean T Jamison, "The Effects of Education Quantity and Quality on Child and Adult Mortality: Their Magnitude and Their Value," World Bank, November 20, 2017. https://www.ncbi.nlm.nih.gov/books/NBK525273/

UNICEF, "Girls' education: A lifeline to development," https://www .unicef.org/sowc96/ngirls.htm

OPPOSING
VIEWPOINTS®
SERIES

CHAPTER 3

How Does Racial Discrimination Lead to Inequities in Education?

Chapter Preface

Because of historical and current systemic racism, a disproportionate number of people of color live in poorer neighborhoods. Funding for public schools is typically tied to local taxes, so schools in poor neighborhoods have less funding. In these districts, schools are larger, class sizes are larger, teachers are less experienced, and materials are of lower quality. When students of color don't perform as well as white students, the differences can be explained by poverty and school quality. However, many Americans believe that every young person has an equal opportunity, so success or failure is up to the individual.

To counteract historical racism, schools need to be equally funded in every neighborhood. Then school districts need to go farther to make sure they are supporting every student. Students can only succeed with well-trained teachers and supports that address individual student needs. Students who are not fluent in English need support so they can catch up to their peers. Teachers and school districts need to develop curricula that supports diversity. These lessons should address the broad diversity of history, culture, and beliefs, without treating white culture as mainstream and other cultures as exceptions to the norm.

Some educational systems are attempting to make these changes. They provide examples that other school districts can follow. Changing the entire structure of education is challenging, but that may be necessary to support equity for students of every race, ethnic group, and background. The viewpoints in this chapter explore some of the issues relating to race and ethnicity in educational equity.

> *"Americans are far more concerned about, and willing to address, wealth-based gaps than race- and ethnicity-based gaps."*

Americans Underestimate Racism in Education

Jon Valant

In the following viewpoint Jon Valant, an expert in K-12 education policy, explores American attitudes about race. He describes a study that found many Americans do not believe discrimination has hurt black students. The author notes some aspects of structural racism that make it harder for black children to succeed. Some of these are societal, while others are specific to the educational system. Equity in education will not be achieved without addressing the racism inherent in educational systems and society. Jon Valant is a senior fellow at the Brookings Institution, a nonprofit public policy organization.

As you read, consider the following questions:

1. What percent of Americans thought racial discrimination affected test scores?
2. How do school systems reinforce racism?
3. What is the problem with using the term "achievement gap"?

A few years ago, I ran a study with a colleague, Daniel Newark, of how Americans think about test score gaps in education. It featured a survey experiment with a nationally representative sample of adults. The study design let us test for differences in how Americans see Black-white, Hispanic-white, and wealthy-poor gaps. The study's main finding was that Americans are far more concerned about, and willing to address, wealth-based gaps than race- and ethnicity-based gaps.

The finding that has stuck with me the most, though, came from a question about how people explain the gaps that exist today. We asked, "How much of the difference in test scores between white students and Black students can be explained by discrimination against Blacks or injustices in society?" Nearly half (44%) of respondents chose "None." Only 10% chose "A great deal."

That 44% figure still feels stunning, and plainly wrong—especially in the aftermath of George Floyd's killing. We are a country only a century-and-a-half removed from the enslavement of African Americans and its accompanying anti-literacy laws, which prohibited teaching slaves to read and write. The end of that era led not to some type of egalitarian or meritocratic society—or any sincere, sustained attempt to get there—but rather to the Jim Crow laws and de jure segregation of yesterday and the de facto segregation and structural racism of today. We are not a country in which current disparities just reflect how hard different groups of people are trying. Yet respondents to our survey were far more inclined to attribute gaps to perceived deficiencies in Black parenting and student motivation than to these profound inequities.

I don't know exactly what attitudes and experiences led to those responses. Undoubtedly, many reflect individual prejudices and failures of empathy. But I also worry that the manifestations of structural racism have become such a fixed, omnipresent part of the educational landscape that it is hard for many of us to see them.

Some of those manifestations are not explicitly in education policy or practice, but they affect students nonetheless. There are exclusionary zoning policies that keep families that can't afford

POVERTY, NOT RACE, FUELS THE ACHIEVEMENT GAP

Researchers found that highly segregated districts had sizable achievement gaps, and the rate of the gap grew faster as students progressed from 3rd to 8th grades. Consider the school districts in Atlanta and Baltimore. Both are highly segregated by race and both have large test-score gaps between black and white students. Atlanta is about 75 percent black and 15 percent white; Baltimore's student population is about 82 percent black and 8 percent white.

But in Atlanta, the test-score gap between white and black children is nearly five grade levels, and in Baltimore, the test-score gap is two grade levels, according to the tool developed by Stanford.

The interactive tool shows that black students in Baltimore attend schools that are relatively more affluent than black students in Atlanta. In Baltimore, black schools are 15 percent poorer than the schools attended by white students. In Atlanta, those schools are 56 percent poorer than those attended by white students.

In contrast, Detroit, which is 83 percent black and about 2 percent white, has an achievement gap of less than a grade level between black and white students. But both groups are scoring more than two grade levels below national averages, and both groups are attending schools classified as high poverty.

"Whether your child is white or black, that [high-poverty] school is likely to be much less effective," Reardon said.

"Poverty, Not Race, Fuels the Achievement Gap," by Christina A. Samuels, EducationWeek, October 1, 2019.

single-family homes out of high-performing school districts; tax policies that prevent Black wealth accumulation (and corresponding spending on educational resources); and mass-incarceration practices that remove parents from children's homes and strain those left behind.

Other manifestations are direct matters of education policy and practice. Some are subtle decisions that happen largely out of sight, day after day, like missed opportunities to assign students of color to advanced coursework and excessive discipline practices that send misguided messages. Others are there for us to see: funding levels that leave many high-poverty schools inadequately resourced; attendance boundaries that erect barriers to desirable schools; and test-based accountability measures that stack the deck against high-poverty schools by emphasizing student proficiency over growth.

If there's a silver lining for education in the simultaneous crises of COVID-19 and police brutality, maybe it's an increased public willingness—however fleeting—to take a closer look at our education systems and the countless inequities they inherit, reproduce, and create. Of course, not everyone will want to look. Some will, though, and perhaps they will see just how defining those inequities are and what we could do about them.

Part of the responsibility for clearer vision lies with the education community, which must speak clearly and honestly about the depth and causes of educational inequity. A growing chorus of scholars—including Gloria Ladson-Billings, Prudence Carter, and Kevin Welner—argues that we have done a poor job of conceptualizing and communicating about inequities. In particular, the term "achievement gap," while useful in increasing public recognition of a problem, connotes a failure of low-scoring students (who do not or cannot "achieve") rather than a societal failure in creating the opportunity gaps that produce those scores. An interesting new paper by David Quinn shows that an "achievement gap" framing can, though does not always, lead people to underestimate Black students' performance—a topic that warrants further study.

Neither the COVID-19 outbreak nor the national outcry over police brutality is, at its core, an education story. But the issues surfaced by those crises are familiar. Education rarely has a lurid moment—what political scientists call a "focusing event"—that, while horrific, can draw attention to an issue and mobilize action. When we do, like the Parkland shooting, it seldom points directly at issues of race and inequality. Rather, moments of educational inequity happen quietly, day after day, in places like classrooms and school-board meeting rooms, often at the hands of people who mean no harm.

In many ways, it's this banality that feels so dangerous. It's that so much of the problem lies in plain sight and still can be so difficult for many of us to see. Hopefully the circumstances of the moment will help us see those problems, and their solutions, more clearly.

> "Black, Indigenous, and other non-
> Black students of color attend schools
> that are statistically more likely
> to be under-resourced, outdated,
> and in many cases hazardous to
> their health."

Systemic Racism in Education Is a Root Cause of Many Other Inequities

Roby Chatterji

In the following viewpoint Roby Chatterji outlines three primary trouble spots that black communities face in their public schools: funding, surveillance and policing, and district segregation. These contribute to lower quality educational experiences that can impact the communities in broader ways. The author looks at the Black Lives Matter movement to argue that newly energized allies should work with black communities to fight perceived systemic racial inequities in education. The author believes these inequities are so deep rooted that it will take the power and privilege of allies who are not black to lend their support and advocate for change to local and state governments. Roby Chatterji is a senior policy analyst for K-12 education at the Center for American Progress.

"Fighting Systemic Racism in K-12 Education: Helping Allies Move from the Keyboard to the School Board," by Roby Chatterji, Center for American Progress, July 8, 2020. Reprinted by permission.

As you read, consider the following questions:

1. According to the viewpoint, what are three ways allies can use their privilege to help people of color receive equitable education?
2. How does the presence of police officers in schools affect black students versus white students?
3. How are parents in Arlington, Virginia, working together, according to the author?

The nationwide uprisings against police brutality in the past few months have led to a significant shift in conversations and attitudes about racial inequities in America. While it may be premature to say that these conversations signal an awakening, books about race and racism are topping bestseller lists; millions of posts on social media are proclaiming that Black Lives Matter; and Americans in at least 1,700 communities across all 50 states and Washington, D.C., are marching in the streets to protest generations of racial injustice.

The killings of Ahmaud Arbery, Breonna Taylor, George Floyd, Rayshard Brooks, and others have galvanized calls and increased support for dramatic changes to policing and criminal justice policies. Many Black leaders and Black-led groups in communities across the country have been working for these changes for decades. It is critically important for newly energized allies, especially those who are not Black, to go beyond hashtag activism and enter this work by listening to the voices of community members and educating themselves on the history, causes, and consequences of systemic racism in the United States.

Allies should also work with Black communities to support efforts to combat structural racism in education, housing, and other social policies. Their opposition, silence, or lack of engagement in these efforts can contribute to the perpetuation of inequities and further limit access to opportunities for communities that are Black, Indigenous, and people of color (BIPOC). Because systemic racism in education is a root cause of so many other inequities that BIPOC face, it is critical that allies stand shoulder to shoulder with these communities in calling for large-scale changes to the US education system. Particularly because education is often thought of as a local concern or personal matter for parents and families, it is especially important that allies lift their voices for BIPOC communities to ensure that the call for change is unified and focused. This column details three ways in which allies should leverage their influence and power beyond social media to combat systemic racism in education.

1. Advocate for Equitable Funding

Money matters in education, with multiple studies showing that increasing funding improves outcomes while cuts hurt them. Still, the United States' school funding systems remain inequitable, disproportionately shortchanging BIPOC students. More than 35 percent of public school revenue comes from property taxes that favor and stabilize funding in wealthier areas, while other communities must rely on more volatile state revenues. This is one reason why predominantly nonwhite school districts across the country annually receive $23 billion less than their predominantly white counterparts.

Black, Indigenous, and other non-Black students of color attend schools that are statistically more likely to be under-resourced, outdated, and in many cases hazardous to their health. Last month, the US Government Accountability Office released a report that estimated more than half of the nation's public school districts needed to update or entirely replace multiple systems, such as HVAC or plumbing, in their school buildings—and many of these districts are concentrated in high-poverty areas. If left unaddressed, these infrastructure problems could pose significant air quality issues, contribute to exacerbating asthma and chronic absenteeism in students, and negatively affect students' academic performance. Notably, higher-poverty districts have less local revenue than low-poverty districts to fund the capital construction costs of addressing these kinds of repairs.

While state funding offsets some of these local disparities, it is not enough. As a result of the Great Recession of 2008, most states significantly cut their education funding—an action shown to have disproportionately affected higher-poverty districts. A number of states still had not restored their education funding to prerecession levels years after the recession ended. Now, in the wake of the COVID-19 crisis, states are once again forecasting massive cuts to their education budgets because of historic shortfalls in income and sales tax revenue.

Allies have a role to play in ensuring that states use stabilization funds—federal funding allocated to states for education purposes to offset their depleted revenue—to prevent these cuts. They should call for increased investments in education as well as fairer and more transparent funding policies at the state and local levels to make sure that capital projects, programs, and overall spending are equitable in schools that serve large numbers of BIPOC students. Organizations such as Gwinnett StoPP and other members of PEER Partners, as well as the Maryland Fair Funding Coalition, include BIPOC-led organizations actively working to advance these efforts.

2. Advocate for Less Policing and Surveillance of Students

Within six months of the deadly 2018 school shooting in Parkland, Florida, legislatures in 26 states allocated nearly $960 million for security upgrades and the addition of police officers to school campuses. While gun violence in schools must be prevented, there is evidence that increased policing and surveillance do not effectively address the threat of gun violence in schools. Black students in particular feel less safe in the presence of police and are more likely to be policed than they are to be protected.

According to data from the US Department of Education's Office for Civil Rights, Black, Hispanic male, and American Indian students face higher rates of school disciplinary consequences such as suspension and expulsion than white students, and they are also subject to more interactions with police in schools in the form of contraband sweeps, interrogations, physical restraints, and arrests. Black students are also more likely to be subjected to social media surveillance and the use of biased artificial intelligence and facial recognition technology.

Additionally, recent data show that approximately 1.7 million students attend schools with police officers but no counselors; 3 million students attend schools with police but no nurses; 6 million students attend schools with police but no psychologist; and 10 million students attend schools with police but no social workers. Middle and high schools with higher concentrations of law enforcement officers compared with mental health staff are more likely to be in areas that serve primarily Black students.

Allies could join one of the many youth- and parent-led BIPOC groups that are part of the Dignity in Schools Campaign to advocate for more counselors, nurses, and social workers in schools instead of increased police presence and security. They should also demand transparency about school discipline data and policies in their local communities to ensure that students' civil rights are not being violated.

3. Advocate to End De-Facto Segregation Through School and District Boundaries

Sixty-six years ago, the unanimous *Brown v. Board of Education* decision declared school segregation unconstitutional, but many public districts and schools remain segregated by race and socioeconomic status today. In many cases, this was an intentional result of the design of school district and neighborhood school assignment boundaries. Since 2000, for example, 128 communities in states from Maine to Utah have attempted to secede from larger school districts. The secession of wealthier and whiter areas takes local tax revenue from districts and increases the number of schools that are racially segregated.

Debates about opportunity hoarding are not limited to particular regions or states. Even in areas that champion their diversity, such as Montgomery County, Maryland—which borders Washington, D.C.—the mere idea of analyzing school attendance boundaries or reassignment plans has caused an uproar. White and Asian parents have protested that any changes to school boundaries that would reduce high concentrations of students from low-income families is unfair to parents who have "worked hard" to live in more affluent neighborhoods. In Howard County, Maryland, a superintendent's plan to reassign students to alleviate crowding and create greater socioeconomic equity resulted in fervent opposition and even a death threat. In addition, the use of screening tests and biased admissions practices for gifted and talented programs in elementary grades and selective middle and high schools have historically woefully underrepresented BIPOC students.

Allies should join with their BIPOC neighbors and show up to their local school board meetings to push for school boundaries and selection criteria that are designed with a race-equity lens. These reforms would ensure that students are not locked out of opportunities based on where they live. In Arlington, Virginia, wealthy and white parents are working with Latinx parents to protest the move of a dual-language immersion school to an area that would be more difficult for Latinx families to attend. Likewise, in Brooklyn, New York, parents of all backgrounds worked together to eliminate gifted tracking programs in favor of enrichment programs available to all students. Allies should also call on their state legislatures and local school boards to create policies that ensure equitable access to rigorous and advanced coursework for all students.

What Lies Ahead

Black communities face injustices that extend beyond the horrifying examples of police killings that have led to calls for big changes to police funding, structures, and policies. Combating the pervasive and deeply rooted forms of systemic racism will require allies—including those in affluent communities—to speak up and speak out.

From the lack of adequate mental health services to inequitable access to advanced and rigorous coursework to unhealthy school buildings, education systems disproportionately fail Black students. Allies can play a role in breaking down these barriers by pushing for change at both state capitols and local school board meetings. They must be vocally supportive of education funding systems that target dollars where they are needed most in order to ensure that opportunities are not restricted based on where people live.

Education budgets are statements of values and should reflect a material commitment to racial equity in schools, not just lip service to diversity. BIPOC students simply cannot afford spending cuts, particularly at a time when they are disproportionately experiencing the worst effects of COVID-19, which will require additional supports and services. Rather than enhanced police and security theater, Black students need more voices calling for equitable resources in schools. Allies must support equitable and diverse schools that improve access to opportunities for BIPOC students and students from low-income families. Parents from affluent communities would not stay silent if their children's public schools were not equitably funded, so they should not remain silent for other children.

> "Despite stark differences in funding, teacher quality, curriculum, and class sizes, the prevailing view is that if students do not achieve, it is their own fault."

Schools Are Not All Equal

Linda Darling-Hammond

In the following viewpoint Linda Darling-Hammond explores attitudes toward affirmative action. Affirmative action is the practice of favoring people belonging to groups that have suffered discrimination in the past. Many people now believe everyone has an equal opportunity, so there is no need for affirmative action. However, this author argues, minority children still have unequal access to important educational resources. To provide students of color with equal opportunities, they need equity in education. Linda Darling-Hammond is founding president of the Learning Policy Institute.

As you read, consider the following questions:

1. How does the US educational system compare to other industrialized countries when it comes to equality?
2. How does the wealth of a school district affect funding?
3. When school funding approaches equality, what happens to student achievement?

"Unequal Opportunity: Race and Education," by Linda Darling-Hammond, The Brookings Institution, March 1, 1998. Reprinted by permission.

W.E.B. DuBois was right about the problem of the 21st century. The color line divides us still. In recent years, the most visible evidence of this in the public policy arena has been the persistent attack on affirmative action in higher education and employment. From the perspective of many Americans who believe that the vestiges of discrimination have disappeared, affirmative action now provides an unfair advantage to minorities. From the perspective of others who daily experience the consequences of ongoing discrimination, affirmative action is needed to protect opportunities likely to evaporate if an affirmative obligation to act fairly does not exist. And for Americans of all backgrounds, the allocation of opportunity in a society that is becoming ever more dependent on knowledge and education is a source of great anxiety and concern.

At the center of these debates are interpretations of the gaps in educational achievement between white and non-Asian minority students as measured by standardized test scores. The presumption that guides much of the conversation is that equal opportunity now exists; therefore, continued low levels of achievement on the part of minority students must be a function of genes, culture, or a lack of effort and will (see, for example, Richard Herrnstein and Charles Murray's *The Bell Curve* and Stephan and Abigail Thernstrom's *America in Black and White*).

The assumptions that undergird this debate miss an important reality: educational outcomes for minority children are much more a function of their unequal access to key educational resources, including skilled teachers and quality curriculum, than they are a function of race. In fact, the US educational system is one of the most unequal in the industrialized world, and students routinely receive dramatically different learning opportunities based on their social status. In contrast to European and Asian nations that fund schools centrally and equally, the wealthiest 10 percent of US school districts spend nearly 10 times more than the poorest 10 percent, and spending ratios of 3 to 1 are common within states. Despite stark differences in funding, teacher quality, curriculum, and class sizes, the prevailing view is that if students do not achieve, it is their own fault. If we are ever to get beyond the problem of the color line, we must confront and address these inequalities.

The Nature of Educational Inequality

Americans often forget that as late as the 1960s most African-American, Latino, and Native American students were educated in wholly segregated schools funded at rates many times lower than those serving whites and were excluded from many higher education institutions entirely. The end of legal segregation followed by efforts to equalize spending since 1970 has made a substantial difference for student achievement. On every major national test, including the National Assessment of Educational Progress, the gap in minority and white students' test scores narrowed substantially between 1970 and 1990, especially for elementary school students. On the Scholastic Aptitude Test (SAT), the scores of African-American students climbed 54 points between 1976 and 1994, while those of white students remained stable.

Even so, educational experiences for minority students have continued to be substantially separate and unequal. Two-thirds of minority students still attend schools that are predominantly minority, most of them located in central cities and funded well below those in neighboring suburban districts. Recent analyses of data prepared for school finance cases in Alabama, New Jersey, New York, Louisiana, and Texas have found that on every tangible measure—from qualified teachers to curriculum offerings—schools serving greater numbers of students of color had significantly fewer resources than schools serving mostly white students. As William L. Taylor and Dianne Piche noted in a 1991 report to Congress: Inequitable systems of school finance inflict disproportionate harm on minority and economically disadvantaged students. On an inter-state basis, such students are concentrated in states, primarily in the South, that have the lowest capacities to finance public education. On an intra-state basis, many of the states with the widest disparities in educational expenditures are large industrial states. In these states, many minorities and economically disadvantaged students are located in property-poor urban districts which fare the worst in educational expenditures (or) in rural districts which suffer from fiscal inequity.

Jonathan Kozol's 1991 *Savage Inequalities* described the striking differences between public schools serving students of color in urban settings and their suburban counterparts, which typically spend twice as much per student for populations with many fewer special needs. Contrast MacKenzie High School in Detroit, where word processing courses are taught without word processors because the school cannot afford them, or East St. Louis Senior High School, whose biology lab has no laboratory tables or usable dissecting kits, with nearby suburban schools where children enjoy a computer hookup to Dow Jones to study stock transactions and science laboratories that rival those in some industries. Or contrast Paterson, New Jersey, which could not afford the qualified teachers needed to offer foreign language courses to most high school students, with Princeton, where foreign languages begin in elementary school.

Even within urban school districts, schools with high concentrations of low-income and minority students receive fewer instructional resources than others. And tracking systems exacerbate these inequalities by segregating many low-income and minority students within schools. In combination, these policies leave minority students with fewer and lower-quality books, curriculum materials, laboratories, and computers; significantly larger class sizes; less qualified and experienced teachers; and less access to high-quality curriculum. Many schools serving low-income and minority students do not even offer the math and science courses needed for college, and they provide lower-quality teaching in the classes they do offer. It all adds up.

What Difference Does It Make?

Since the 1966 Coleman report, Equality of Educational Opportunity, another debate has waged as to whether money makes a difference to educational outcomes. It is certainly possible to spend money ineffectively; however, studies that have developed more sophisticated measures of schooling show how money, properly spent, makes a difference. Over the past 30 years, a large body of research has shown that four factors consistently influence student achievement: all else equal, students perform better if they are educated in smaller schools where they are well known (300 to 500 students is optimal), have smaller class sizes (especially at the elementary level), receive a challenging curriculum, and have more highly qualified teachers.

Minority students are much less likely than white children to have any of these resources. In predominantly minority schools, which most students of color attend, schools are large (on average, more than twice as large as predominantly white schools and reaching 3,000 students or more in most cities); on average, class sizes are 15 percent larger overall (80 percent larger for non-special education classes); curriculum offerings and materials are lower in quality; and teachers are much less qualified in terms of levels of education, certification, and training in the fields they teach. And in integrated schools, as UCLA professor Jeannie Oakes described in the 1980s and Harvard professor Gary Orfield's research has recently confirmed, most minority students are segregated in lower-track classes with larger class sizes, less qualified teachers, and lower-quality curriculum.

Research shows that teachers' preparation makes a tremendous difference to children's learning. In an analysis of 900 Texas school districts, Harvard economist Ronald Ferguson found that teachers' expertise—as measured by scores on a licensing examination, master's degrees, and experienc—was the single most important determinant of student achievement, accounting for roughly 40 percent of the measured variance in students' reading and math achievement gains in grades 1-12. After controlling for socioeconomic status, the large disparities in achievement between black and white students were almost entirely due to differences in the qualifications of their teachers. In combination, differences in teacher expertise and class sizes accounted for as much of the measured variance in achievement as did student and family background.

Ferguson and Duke economist Helen Ladd repeated this analysis in Alabama and again found sizable influences of teacher qualifications and smaller class sizes on achievement gains in math and reading. They found that more of the difference between the high- and low-scoring districts was explained by teacher qualifications and class sizes than by poverty, race, and parent education.

Meanwhile, a Tennessee study found that elementary school students who are assigned to ineffective teachers for three years in a row score nearly 50 percentile points lower on achievement tests than those assigned to highly effective teachers over the same period. Strikingly, minority students are about half as likely to be assigned to the most effective teachers and twice as likely to be assigned to the least effective.

Minority students are put at greatest risk by the American tradition of allowing enormous variation in the qualifications of teachers. The National Commission on Teaching and America's Future found that new teachers hired without meeting certification standards (25 percent of all new teachers) are usually assigned to teach the most disadvantaged students in low-income and high-minority schools, while the most highly educated new teachers are hired largely by wealthier schools. Students in poor or predominantly minority schools are much less likely to have teachers who are fully qualified or hold higher-level degrees. In schools with the highest minority enrollments, for example, students have less than a 50 percent chance of getting a math or science teacher with a license and a degree in the field. In 1994, fully one-third of teachers in high-poverty schools taught without a minor in their main field and nearly 70 percent taught without a minor in their secondary teaching field.

Studies of underprepared teachers consistently find that they are less effective with students and that they have difficulty with curriculum development, classroom management, student motivation, and teaching strategies. With little knowledge about how children grow, learn, and develop, or about what to do to support their learning, these teachers are less likely to understand students' learning styles and differences, to anticipate students' knowledge and potential difficulties, or to plan and redirect instruction to meet students' needs. Nor are they likely to see it as their job to do so, often blaming the students if their teaching is not successful.

Teacher expertise and curriculum quality are interrelated, because a challenging curriculum requires an expert teacher. Research has found that both students and teachers are tracked: that is, the most expert teachers teach the most demanding courses to the most advantaged students, while lower-track students assigned to less able teachers receive lower-quality teaching and less demanding material. Assignment to tracks is also related to race: even when grades and test scores are comparable, black students are more likely to be assigned to lower-track, nonacademic classes.

When Opportunity Is More Equal

What happens when students of color do get access to more equal opportunities' Studies find that curriculum quality and teacher skill make more difference to educational outcomes than the initial test scores or racial backgrounds of students. Analyses of national data from both the High School and Beyond Surveys and the National Educational Longitudinal Surveys have demonstrated that, while there are dramatic differences among students of various racial and ethnic groups in course-taking in such areas as math, science, and foreign language, for students with similar course-taking records, achievement test score differences by race or ethnicity narrow substantially.

Robert Dreeben and colleagues at the University of Chicago conducted a long line of studies documenting both the relationship between educational opportunities and student performance and minority students' access to those opportunities. In a comparative study of 300 Chicago first graders, for example, Dreeben found that African-American and white students who had comparable instruction achieved comparable levels of reading skill. But he also found that the quality of instruction given African-American students was, on average, much lower than that given white students, thus creating a racial gap in aggregate achievement at the end of first grade. In fact, the highest-ability group in Dreeben's sample was in a school in a low-income African-American neighborhood. These children, though, learned less during first grade than their white counterparts because their teacher was unable to provide the challenging instruction they deserved.

When schools have radically different teaching forces, the effects can be profound. For example, when Eleanor Armour-Thomas and colleagues compared a group of exceptionally effective elementary schools with a group of low-achieving schools with similar demographic characteristics in New York City, roughly 90 percent of the variance in student reading and mathematics scores at grades 3, 6, and 8 was a function of differences in teacher qualifications. The schools with highly qualified teachers serving large numbers of minority and low-income students performed as well as much more advantaged schools.

Most studies have estimated effects statistically. However, an experiment that randomly assigned seventh grade "at-risk"students to remedial, average, and honors mathematics classes found that the at-risk students who took the honors class offering a pre-algebra curriculum ultimately outperformed all other students of similar backgrounds. Another study compared African-American high school youth randomly placed in public housing in the Chicago suburbs with city-placed peers of equivalent income and initial academic attainment and found that the suburban students, who attended largely white and better-funded schools, were substantially more likely to take challenging courses, perform well academically, graduate on time, attend college, and find good jobs.

What Can Be Done?

This state of affairs is not inevitable. Last year the National Commission on Teaching and America's Future issued a blueprint for a comprehensive set of policies to ensure a "caring, competent, and qualified teacher for every child," as well as schools organized to support student success. Twelve states are now working directly with the commission on this agenda, and others are set to join this year. Several pending bills to overhaul the federal Higher Education Act would ensure that highly qualified teachers are recruited and prepared for students in all schools. Federal policymakers can develop incentives, as they have in medicine, to guarantee well-prepared teachers in shortage fields and high-need locations. States can equalize education spending, enforce higher teaching standards, and reduce teacher shortages, as Connecticut, Kentucky, Minnesota, and North Carolina have already done. School districts can reallocate resources from administrative superstructures and special add-on programs to support better-educated teachers who offer a challenging curriculum in smaller schools and classes, as restructured schools as far apart as New York and San Diego have done. These schools, in communities where children are normally written off to lives of poverty, welfare dependency, or incarceration, already produce much higher levels of achievement for students of color, sending more than 90 percent of their students to college. Focusing on what matters most can make a real difference in what children have the opportunity to learn. This, in turn, makes a difference in what communities can accomplish.

An Entitlement to Good Teaching

The common presumption about educational inequality—that it resides primarily in those students who come to school with inadequate capacities to benefit from what the school has to offer—continues to hold wide currency because the extent of inequality in opportunities to learn is largely unknown. We do not currently operate schools on the presumption that students might be entitled to decent teaching and schooling as a matter of course. In fact, some state and local defendants have countered school finance and desegregation cases with assertions that such remedies are not required unless it can be proven that they will produce equal outcomes. Such arguments against equalizing opportunities to learn have made good on DuBois's prediction that the problem of the 20th century would be the problem of the color line.

But education resources do make a difference, particularly when funds are used to purchase well-qualified teachers and high-quality curriculum and to create personalized learning communities in which children are well known. In all of the current sturm und drang about affirmative action, "special treatment," and the other high-volatility buzzwords for race and class politics in this nation, I would offer a simple starting point for the next century s efforts: no special programs, just equal educational opportunity.

> *"Counteracting racism is an essential step in supporting students of color to access their full potential."*

Work Together to Counteract Racism

Sarah Caverly and David Osher

In the following viewpoint Sarah Caverly and David Osher explore ways educational systems can address inherent racism. The authors use the case study of one school system, in Austin, Texas, to show how actively addressing racism can affect outcomes. Teachers, other school staff, students, and parents may all need to be involved for optimal success. If this school district shows improvement with the new policies, that could create a model for other schools to follow. Sarah Caverly is a principle researcher at the American Institutes for Research. David Osher is vice president and institute fellow at the American Institutes for Research.

As you read, consider the following questions:

1. Why is it important for students to have teachers from their own races, according to the viewpoint?
2. How can antiracism training help school staff better support students of color?
3. How can students be involved in antiracism efforts?

Caverly, S., & Osher, D. (2021, January 25). "Why a system level approach is needed to counterracism within the education system." American Institutes for Research. https://www.air.org/resource/why-system-levelapproach-needed-counter-racism-within-education-system. Reprinted with permission from the American Institutes for Research.

The death of George Floyd, along with racial inequities exacerbated by the global coronavirus pandemic, pushed racial justice issues to the forefront of our conversations in 2020. While the harmful impacts of racism on the lives and opportunities of Black, Indigenous, and people of color are well-known, racism persists in the everyday practices and policies of our organizations and institutions, including our education system.

Here are just some of the effects of systemic racism within education.

- Black students are less likely than white students to have access to college-ready courses, and even when Black students do have access to honors or Advanced Placement courses, they are vastly underrepresented.
- Research also shows systemic bias in teacher expectations, with non-Black teachers having lower expectations of Black students compared with Black teachers.
- Black students more frequently attend schools with teachers who are less qualified, have lower salaries, and are new to the field.
- Black students spend less time in the classroom due to disparate exclusionary discipline consequences, which further hinders their access to quality education.

Approaching Anti-Racism in a Systemic Way

Counteracting racism is an essential step in supporting students of color to access their full potential. To truly transform the current landscape, change is needed at the systemic level; this in turn supports and reinforces change at the individual level. Systemic change highlights the interrelationships and interdependencies of the educational system. Unless we fully recognize how the system— replete with institutionalized racism and privilege—is embedded within the solution, we will only be able to achieve minimal shifts for young people and their families.

Our collective refocusing on racism in 2020 sparked a deeper discussion on dismantling and rebuilding a stronger educational system, one that would support and engage all students through culturally responsive practices and policies. Several state education agencies and school districts began shifting toward achieving equity for all students by including a whole child approach and applying an equity lens. In a few instances, school districts elevated the importance of equity by establishing an equity office. However, we have yet to achieve true equity, and we must do more.

Systemic Changes in Austin

The Austin Independent School District (ISD), led by anti-racism expert and consultant Angela Ward, Ph.D., is a prime example of how a school district is addressing issues of persistent racism at the system level. (Photo, right: Austin ISD education leaders attend a CP&I training.)

Within Austin ISD, almost 60 percent of students are Latinx, approximately 7 percent are Black, and 30 percent are white. As often is the case, school populations reflect patterns of segregation across the city, and the majority of teachers are white women. While, in recent years, Austin ISD has improved student test scores and hired and retained more qualified teachers, these improvements are unevenly distributed and tend to occur in primarily affluent, well-educated, largely white neighborhoods.

Austin ISD is not unique in its student demographics, but it is unique in its approach and dedication to implementing equity-focused social and emotional learning programs. Over the past 10 years, Ward has supported and initiated system-level changes within Austin ISD to provide safe and supportive schools for all students and families—especially those of color.

Austin ISD's Cultural Proficiency and Inclusiveness (CP&I) team, led by Ward, includes Culturally Responsive Restorative Practice Associates, who work across 11 schools; CP&I specialists; and a coordinator for restorative practices. Many of the team's ongoing efforts focus on the system level and are sustained through deep engagement with administrators, educators, and families. Grant programs at the local, state, and federal level support the team's work.

Here are a few ways in which the CP&I team works at both the system and individual levels to establish safe, supportive learning environments for all:

1. Initiating Change Among District and School Leaders and Staff

As the CP&I team has expanded its reach, more district and campus leaders and school staff began to understand how their personal lens affects how they make decisions for the students and families in their care. Austin ISD staff have engaged in anti-racist dialogue and identified and removed barriers that stand in their way of helping students succeed.

2. Establishing Restorative Justice

In 2017, Austin ISD received a Culturally Responsive Restorative Practices (CRRP) grant through the US Department of Education and a second grant from the Office of Juvenile Justice and Delinquency Prevention in 2019 to support their restorative practice efforts. CRRP, differing from traditional approaches to school climate and discipline, supports the safety, well-being, and success of students by nurturing positive relationships, fostering school connectedness, and building social and emotional competencies. Specifically, restorative practices not only provide effective responses when incidents of disruption and harm have occurred (i.e., viable alternatives to removing students from classroom activities), but also offers methods and a framework for teachers and administrators to work with young people to build respectful relationships. To facilitate this process, restorative practice associates are embedded within each of the 11 Austin schools participating in the grants. AIR serves as the external evaluator for Austin ISD's CRRP grant program and is examining implementation and district data to measure student and teacher outcomes. So far, AIR has focused on providing formative feedback to the development team and will focus on student and teacher outcomes during the 2020-2021 school year.

3. Involving Students in Leading Anti-Racism Efforts

More recently, the CP&I team established the Student Race Equity Leadership course for students. This leadership course, operating in two schools with plans to expand, is a yearlong elective course with the goal of increasing students' racial literacy, sense of agency, and civic responsibility. Participating students say the course has been transformative. After the first pilot of the Race Equity Leadership course in one Austin ISD high school, students have already asserted their agency and voice. For example, students are now engaged in school planning meetings and engage educators in discussions of race and culture of their school. On Dec. 11, 2020, Austin ISD launched the first student equity council.

4. Engaging Parents in Conversations on Race

Starting in summer 2020, the Race Equity Council, an advisory group to the CP&I team—that includes volunteer district staff and community members—began engaging Austin ISD families and parents in conversations about race. The team plans to continue this effort.

Next Steps for Austin—and the Education System

While there is limited evidence so far to demonstrate whether the CP&I professional learning sessions and efforts are leading to change in the Austin ISD, the district is undertaking evaluations to measure the influence on school climate, students' experience with racism, teachers' perception, as well as academic achievement.

In the meantime, Austin ISD's continued focus on equity and anti-racism can serve as an example for schools and districts grappling with segregation, a history of racism, and inequity.

> *"Remember, by providing an equitable learning opportunity for ELLs, you are helping to create a safe classroom culture that respects and honors all students and their autonomy."*

English-Language Learners Need Support

Rusul Alrubail

In the following viewpoint Rusul Alrubail addresses education for English-language learners (ELLs). These students are not fluent in English, typically because they come from homes in which English is not spoken. The author argues that ELL students should be assessed for their content skills separately from their language skills. Otherwise, they might fail due to poor English skills, when they actually know the material. ELLs need classrooms that allow them to practice their English skills, and they benefit from certain other accommodations. When ELL students cannot keep up with native English speakers and don't get the proper support, they are sometimes put into special education classes. Rusul Alrubail is an education writer and a student voice advocate.

As you read, consider the following questions:

1. How much growth are we seeing in the number of ELLs in public schools?
2. Why do ELL students need special accommodations?
3. How can teachers help ELLs catch up to their peers?

To understand English-language learners' need for equitable education, we must first look at the dramatic increase in the numbers of ELLs in US public schools. Between 1997-1998 and 2008-2009, the number of ELLs in public schools increased by 51%. However, the general student population only grew by 7% (Center for American Progress). ELLs are the fastest-growing student population with approximately six million currently enrolled in public schools (TESOL International Association).

Consequently, equitable practices both in and out of the classroom must be implemented to ensure that English-language learners get a fair opportunity not only at learning, but also at excelling in learning.

Ensuring Fair Assessment

With all of the standards and testing that teachers have to conduct in the classroom, it's important that we ensure a fair assessment for ELLs. When we assess this population, we must remember to separate language skills from content skills. Some of these language skills include vocabulary, comprehension, phonology, grammar (syntax), and meaning (semantics). Content assessment focuses on whether or not the student was able to grasp the subject matter. Duverger (2005) suggests that "another way of disentangling the effects of language proficiency on content proficiency is to have a double scale of criteria: criteria relating to the content being delivered and criteria relating to the language being used." This is a helpful strategy as it allows the teacher to create some sort of scale or rubric to easily identify the language skills during and after assessment.

Providing Students With Quality Instruction and Resources

To many ELLs, the learning opportunity that they receive is different than their native-speaker counterparts. Research suggests that effective English-language learning classrooms foster a strong environment of collaboration, dialogue, and group engagement. It's important that students have multiple opportunities throughout the day to engage in conversational-style learning with their peers so that they can practice their oral language skills. Working collaboratively also fosters a culture of community in the classroom.

Research shows that ELLs can experience two categories regarding the quality of instruction:

1. Students are not challenged enough in the classroom when it comes to engaging critically through oral or written work (Callahan, 2003; 2005).

2. When students are placed in an English-only classroom, it's harder for them to grasp content and catch up to their peers.

ELLs are often overrepresented in special education classes due to a lack of training in helping teachers identify students' needs and assessment when it comes language skills. "This error comes as a result of the shortage of special educators who are trained to understand issues of bilingualism and second-language development," Ortiz suggests in English language learners with special needs: Effective instructional strategies. To provide the best instructional practices for ELLs, a teacher must be willing to accommodate their learning needs and provide them with equitable learning opportunities.

Resources become a huge aspect in teaching ELLs. Teachers can leverage available resources to help fill in gaps in language. Visit Edutopia's English-Language Learners topic page for more articles about and strategies for leveraging open resources and useful technology in your classroom.

Equitable Accommodations

Some of these accommodations may seem simple, but they can actually make a difference in your students' journey to learning English:

Allow Students to Use a Dictionary and/or Thesaurus. This can help them a great deal in understanding instructions and content to help them answer questions on a test, quiz, or any other form of assessment.

Give students extra time. ELLs often need extra time to decipher and understand the meaning of an assessment's content. They also need extra time to formulate their thoughts and ideas into sentences and paragraphs.

Provide an alternate method of teaching and learning. Whenever possible, provide information, instructions, and content through an alternative method, such as visual or audio. This allows ELLs to connect with the content not just through words but also through other senses. Encourage the use of other methods as well if they're creating the content. For example, multimedia can help them tell a story or write a response.

Allow translations. It's totally fine if students need to write in their first language and then translate into English. By permitting students to do this, you not only ensure them an equitable opportunity at learning, but you also help them catch up to their peers in learning the content and material without leaving them behind.

Teaching ELLs requires a lot of accommodation, understanding, and empathizing on the teacher's part. The students will benefit from an equitable learning environment among their peers, and that can help them to excel not only in learning the language faster, but also in learning the material. Remember, by providing an equitable learning opportunity for ELLs, you are helping to create a safe classroom culture that respects and honors all students and their autonomy.

> *"With less inclusive goals, the aim is for students to gain knowledge, skills, and attitudes sanctioned by the mainstream, with little inclusion of alternatives."*

Diversity Should Be Mainstream

Thomas F. Nelson Laird

In the following viewpoint, Thomas F. Nelson Laird notes that everyone benefits when schools include and support people with diverse backgrounds and ideas. However, the author contends, teachers often do not even consider diversity. Or they do include diversity, but they do it in a way that makes white culture seem like the standard and "normal." It is important to make students feel included by incorporating diversity smoothly into teaching, Laird explains. The author addresses the different ways courses can be developed to include or exclude diversity. Thomas F. Nelson Laird is a professor at Indiana University Bloomington whose work focuses on improving teaching and learning at colleges and universities.

As you read, consider the following questions:

1. How does society benefit when diversity is supported in education?
2. What happens when white teachers develop courses without considering diversity?
3. Are people of color and women more likely to include diversity in their classes?

As institutions seek to improve all students' success, the inclusion of people with diverse backgrounds, ideas, and methods of teaching and learning is an educational imperative. Such inclusion simultaneously (1) creates more equitable opportunities for students from marginalized groups to participate in higher education and (2) promotes the kinds of outcomes for all students that employers and society need, such as complex thinking skills, the ability to work across difference, increased civic participation, and decreased prejudice (see, for example, National Leadership Council 2007).

Faculty members often recognize that inclusion is a key to learning. Even among students who have access to an educational experience, those who feel excluded from the full experience struggle to learn as well as those who feel included (Hurtado et al. 1999). To create an inclusive learning environment throughout the curriculum and in all fields, all faculty members should consider how they are incorporating diversity into their courses and how they can be more inclusive in their teaching.

Incorporating diversity into one's teaching takes time and depends on the specifics of the situation (who is teaching which students, and in what context). Faculty members do not need simple solutions that may not work for their circumstances. Therefore, I offer the framework described below not as a prescription, but as a guide for faculty seeking their own ways of including diversity in their courses.

A Diversity Inclusivity Framework

Table 1 illustrates a framework for evaluating how the different elements of a course are more or less inclusive of diversity. On the left is a list of nine elements that are key to course design and delivery. To the right of each element is a continuum that illustrates how the element can vary from not inclusive to fully inclusive.

Table 1: Diversity Inclusivity Framework

ELEMENT	INCLUSIVITY CONTINUUM					
Purpose/ goals	Prepare students	→	Prepare students for diverse experiences	→	Prepare students to actively engage in a diverse society	
Content	Monocultural	→	Additive	→	Multicultural	
Foundations/ perspectives	Unexplored	→	Exposed	→	Multiple foundations/ perspectives examined	
Learners	Passive acceptors	→	Participants with some learning needs	→	Collaborators with diverse learning needs	
Instructor(s)	Unexplored views, biases, values	→	Exploring own views, biases, values	→	Understands own views, biases, values	
Pedagogy	Filling students with knowledge	→	Transitional— using varied techniques	→	Critical/ equity oriented	
Environment	Ignored	→	Inclusive	→	Empowering	
Assessment/ evaluation	"Standard"	→	Mixed methods	→	Methods suited to student diversity	
Adjustment	Adjustment to cover material	→	Adjustment to some needs of students	→	Adjustment to divers needs of students	

To create the framework, I reviewed models that describe aspects of multicultural education, phases of multicultural curricular change, or planning processes for multicultural course change. I referred to models primarily in multicultural and diversity education literature, but also in other areas. Several of these models suggested a continuum, but most focused at the level of an entire course or curriculum, allowing for overemphasis on goals/ purposes and content. Focusing instead at the course element level (something done by only a few authors, such as Kitano [1997]) allows the continuum to vary in nature from element to element and places equal emphasis on each element.

Among the models I reviewed, courses at the noninclusive end of the spectrum demonstrate what is (or was) traditional practice: with regard to race, white people "neither study people of color nor notice that they have not" (McIntosh 1990, 6) and faculty teach in "standard" ways without considering whether their approaches work for particular subgroups of students. When a course includes diversity to some extent, content about "others" may be added to the course, but in a way that makes nonmainstream groups seem exceptional, deficient, or marginal. On this side of the continuum, the frame of reference remains mainstream-centric (Banks, 2010).

Toward the inclusive end of the continuum, "an enormous shift in consciousness occurs" (McIntosh 1990, 7). Here, mainstream norms, perspectives, and assumptions are brought to light and multiple alternative norms, perspectives, and assumptions are explored (Banks 2010; Green 1989; McIntosh 1990). Within the most inclusive courses, instructors factor in the complex relationships between learning and diversity (Banks 2006, 2010; Schoem et al. 1993).

The nine elements in table 1 come from a subset of models that identify aspects of multicultural education or diversity coursework. When organizing the elements, I referred to Lattuca and Stark's (2009) general model of curriculum planning, which encompasses most of the elements described in the models I consulted. Below, I define each element and explain how it varies along the inclusivity continuum.

Purpose/Goals

A course's purposes or goals represent its intended outcomes. With inclusive goals, the aim is for students to gain the knowledge, attitudes, and skills necessary for participation in a diverse society. With less inclusive goals, the aim is for students to gain knowledge, skills, and attitudes sanctioned by the mainstream, with little inclusion of alternatives.

Content

Course content includes the subject matter covered, the way it is ordered, and the materials used to present it. In courses that include some diversity, the content includes subjects that are ignored in traditional courses or alternative perspectives on traditional subjects. In more inclusive courses, the content reflects the experiences of multiple cultural groups from their own as well as other perspectives.

Foundations/Perspectives

The background characteristics of students and faculty affect their understandings of events (e.g., Columbus's voyages), issues (e.g., domestic violence), and concepts (e.g., justice). A course that includes diverse foundations or perspectives draws on theories that help explain how human differences influence our understanding of a course topic (Banks 2006). As a course's foundations become more inclusive, the number of perspectives and depth of understanding increases, and the foundations and perspectives themselves generally become a part of the course's content (Bell and Griffin 2007).

Learners

At the noninclusive end of the spectrum, student characteristics (e.g., race, gender, class, skill level, and developmental needs) are not taken into account. At the inclusive end, these characteristics are assessed and explored so that other course elements can be designed and adjusted to fit students' learning needs (Bell and Griffin 2007; Schoem et al. 1993).

Instructor(s)

In more inclusive classrooms, the individuals charged with planning and facilitating a course investigate their own identities, biases, and values, and how these may influence the way they operate in the classroom. Inclusive instructors also learn about identities, biases, and values that are different from their own so that the course can rely on multiple perspectives.

Pedagogy

In addition to classroom processes and teaching methods, pedagogy includes the theories and scholarship (e.g., theories of student development and learning) that inform these processes and methods. More inclusive pedagogies account for the fact that not all students are the same, but rather have varied learning needs. At its most inclusive, pedagogy will demonstrate a focus on the learning of diverse students through the interplay of theory and instructional process at a highly developed level.

Classroom Environment

The classroom environment is the space where a course takes place as well as the interactions that occur within that space. It consists of the values, norms, ethos, and experiences of a course. When highly inclusive, the environment should be empowering (Banks 2006), reflective of the diverse backgrounds of students and instructors (Schoem et al. 1993), and structured to support student learning (Bell and Griffin, 2007).

Assessment/Evaluation

Instructors should use a variety of methods, both formal and informal, to assess student characteristics and learning and should also be aware of potential biases in their techniques (Banks 2006; Lattuca and Stark 2009). More inclusive evaluation methods are more sensitive to the various backgrounds of students and the diverse ways students can demonstrate understanding.

Adjustment

In any course, instructors may need to change their plans as assessments reveal new information about students, as student desires or frustrations assert themselves, as incidents occur in class, or as activities require more time than allotted. An instructor who capitalizes on new information can adjust other elements of a course to enhance student learning (Bell and Griffin 2007; Lattuca and Stark 2009). Inclusive adjustments are sensitive to students' diverse learning needs and matched to course goals. Adjustments made despite student needs (e.g., to cover a predetermined amount of material) are noninclusive.

This framework can be applied in a variety of areas, including course design and assessment. In the area of course design, for example, the framework encourages instructors to question and make decisions about the inclusivity of each element when designing or making adjustments to a course. The framework allows for flexibility in which elements a faculty member chooses to address, and in which order (as decisions about one element will affect decisions about the others).

Lessons Learned from Assessing Diversity Inclusivity

In 2007 and 2010, the Faculty Survey of Student Engagement administered survey items focused on diversity inclusivity to US faculty at over one hundred institutions (for detailed findings from the 2007 administration, see Nelson Laird [2011] and Nelson Laird and Engberg [2011]). The results suggested four lessons about including diversity in college courses.

First, while differences by academic field were apparent, many faculty members from all fields reported including diversity in a variety of ways. For example, 57 percent of all faculty respondents indicated that students in their courses gain "quite a bit" or "very much" understanding of how to connect their learning to societal problems or issues. Three-quarters (75 percent) of faculty respondents indicated that they varied their teaching methods "quite a bit" or "very much" to encourage the active participation of all students, and most faculty members (87 percent) indicated that they try "quite a bit" or "very much" to empower students through class participation. These findings suggest that many faculty members are already invested in creating inclusive courses. Therefore, instead of trying to convince faculty members to be inclusive, colleges and universities should spend time and resources helping faculty members find ways to be inclusive in their own particular manner.

Second, including diversity in a course is strongly connected to other indicators of effective educational practices. Faculty members who include diversity in their courses are much more likely to encourage peer interactions across difference, emphasize deep approaches to learning, use active classroom practices, interact with their students, and promote learning outcomes like intellectual and practical skills or personal and social responsibility.

Third, faculty members' perceptions of the curriculum matter. The more faculty members perceive the undergraduate curriculum as inclusive of diversity, the more likely they are to include diversity in their own courses. Combined with the second lesson, this suggests that faculty members and institutional leaders invested in promoting student success should do more to share all that is happening in the curriculum related to the inclusion of diversity.

Fourth, while all kinds of faculty members include diversity into their courses, women and faculty members of color are much more likely than their male and white colleagues to do so. Combined with the other lessons, this suggests that those invested in improving the quality of undergraduate education should encourage faculty search committees to look seriously at female applicants and applicants of color, while also identifying ways to help male and white faculty members find elements of their courses where inclusivity can be improved.

By marshaling faculty creativity as well as higher education research and scholarship, colleges and universities can foster greater inclusivity in the classroom.

References

Banks, James A. 2006. Cultural Diversity and Education: Foundations, Curriculum, and Teaching. 5th ed. Boston, MA: Pearson Education.

————. 2010. "Approaches to Multicultural Curriculum Reform." In Multicultural Education: Issues and Perspectives, edited by James A. Banks and Cherry A. McGee Banks, 7th ed., 233–56. New York: John Wiley & Sons.

Bell, Lee Anne, and Pat Griffin. 2007. "Designing Social Justice Education Courses." In Teaching for Diversity and Social Justice, edited by Maurianne Adams, Lee Anne Bell, and Pat Griffin, 2nd ed., 67–87. New York: Routledge.

Green, Madeleine F., ed. 1989. Minorities on Campus: A Handbook for Enhancing Diversity. Washington, DC: American Council on Education.

Hurtado, Sylvia, Jeffrey Milem, Alma Clayton-Pedersen, and Walter Allen. 1999. Enacting Diverse Learning Environments: Improving the Climate for Racial/Ethnic Diversity in Higher Education. ASHE-ERIC Higher Education Report 26 (8). Washington, DC: The George Washington University Graduate School of Education and Human Development.

Kitano, Margie K. 1997. "What a Course Will Look Like after Multicultural Change." In Multicultural Course Transformation in Higher Education: A Broader Truth, edited by Ann Intili Morey and Margie K. Kitano, 18–34. Boston, MA: Allyn & Bacon.

Lattuca, Lisa R., and Joan S. Stark. 2009. Shaping the College Curriculum: Academic Plans in Context, 2nd ed. San Francisco: Jossey-Bass.

McIntosh, Peggy. 1990. "Interactive Phases of Curricular and Personal Re-vision with Regard to Race." Working Paper 219, Wellesley College Center for Research on Women, Wellesley, MA.

National Leadership Council for Liberal Education and America's Promise. 2007. College Learning for the New Global Century. Washington, DC: Association of American Colleges and Universities.

Nelson Laird, Thomas F. 2011. "Measuring the Diversity Inclusivity of College Courses." Research in Higher Education 52, 572–88.

Nelson Laird, Thomas F., and Mark E. Engberg. 2011. "Establishing Differences between Diversity Requirements and Other Courses with Varying Degrees of Diversity Inclusivity." Journal of General Education 60, 117–37.

Schoem, David, Linda Frankel, Ximena Zúñiga, and Edith A. Lewis. 1993. "The Meaning of Multicultural Teaching: An Introduction." In Multicultural Teaching in the University, edited by David Schoem, Linda Frankel, Ximena Zúñiga, and Edith A. Lewis, 1–12. Westport, CT: Praeger.

Periodical and Internet Sources Bibliography

The following articles have been selected to supplement the diverse views presented in this chapter.

Brigham Young University School of Education, "Multicultural Curriculum," https://education.byu.edu/diversity/curriculum.html

Johnnella E. Butler, "Replacing the Cracked Mirror: The Challenge for Diversity and Inclusion," Association of American Colleges and niversities. https://www.aacu.org/diversitydemocracy/2014/fall/butler

Kathryn Peltier Campbell, "Climates for Diversity: Checking the Barometer," Association of American Colleges and Universities. https://www.aacu.org/diversitydemocracy/2014/fall/editor

Diane Staehr Fenner, "Fair And Square Assessments for ELLs," ASCD, February 2016. http://www.ascd.org/publications/educational-leadership/feb16/vol73/num05/Fair-And-Square-Assessments-for-ELLs.aspx

Kim Fischer, "Systemic Racism Has Led to Education Disparities," Temple Now, June 25, 2020. https://news.temple.edu/news/2020-06-25/systemic-racism-has-led-education-disparities

Britney L. Jones, "Reducing Racism in Schools: The Promise of Anti-Racist Policies," University of Connecticut, September 22, 2020. https://education.uconn.edu/2020/09/22/reducing-racism-in-schools-the-promise-of-anti-racist-policies/#

Lumen Learning, "Education and Inequality," https://courses.lumenlearning.com/boundless-sociology/chapter/education-and-inequality/

Matt Morton, "Myth: Disparities in education are not an issue of race but rather an issue of poverty," Meyer Memorial Trust, August 12, 2019. https://mmt.org/news/myth-disparities-education-are-not-issue-race-rather-issue-poverty

Christina A. Samuels, "Poverty, Not Race, Fuels the Achievement Gap," EdWeek, October 01, 2019. https://www.edweek.org/leadership/poverty-not-race-fuels-the-achievement-gap/2019/10

OPPOSING
VIEWPOINTS®
SERIES

CHAPTER 4

How Does Socioeconomic Status Lead to Differences in Learning?

Chapter Preface

Race and poverty are connected, due to historical and current systemic racism. That can make it challenging to separate the effects of racism from the effects of poverty. It is important for people and organizations attempting school reform to consider both aspects and the way they interact. According to the Children's Defense Fund, a nonprofit organization, nearly 1.3 million children under age 6 were homeless during the last report, in 2016. In addition, almost 1.4 million children enrolled in public schools experienced homelessness during the 2016-2017 school year. Homelessness is defined as living in the streets, in abandoned buildings or cars, in transitional housing, in hotels or motels, or doubled up with family or friends. Children in any of these situations suffer more physical and mental health problems and are less likely to receive treatment.

Even children who have stable homes do not all have the same opportunities. Low-income students are unlikely to participate in the out of school activities available to students from wealthier families. Schools with more low-income families are less likely to provide help with college or career planning. Rural schools may have trouble attracting highly qualified teachers and may not provide the same options as urban schools. Some of these options, such as advanced placement classes, increase a student's chances of getting into certain colleges.

Special government funding exists for schools with larger populations of low-income students. However, critics argue that the money provided is not nearly enough. In addition, it may not be spent in ways that best benefit those low-income students. Money is often spent on activities that have not been shown to increase student outcomes. Without studies to show what does and does not help students succeed, more money will not solve the problem of poor student achievement. Educational equity will not be achieved until all students, regardless of family income, have access to the same opportunities in and out of school.

"Realistically, how much improvement can we expect by adding 5 percent to education spending?"

Schools Need More Money, and the Money Needs to Be Spent More Effectively

Mark Dynarski and Kirsten Kainz

In the following viewpoint Mark Dynarski and Kirsten Kainz argue that the Title I program is not currently effective. While the total amount of money involved sounds like a lot, it breaks down to be not much per student. In addition, the money does not necessarily go to students who are economically disadvantaged. Furthermore, few studies have been done to track the effectiveness of the overall program or specific uses of the money. Much of the funding goes to professional development for teachers, which has not been proven to improve student outcomes. The authors argue that schools need much more funding than they currently receive. They also cite studies that suggest how the money can be spent effectively. Mark Dynarski is the founder and owner of Pemberton Research and a former Brookings expert. Kirsten Kainz is a research associate professor at the University of North Carolina at Chapel Hill's School of Education.

As you read, consider the following questions:

1. How much money does the Title I program provide per student, on average?
2. How much money should be spent per student per year, according to the sources cited?
3. Why has it been hard to track the effectiveness of Title I school support?

The Elementary and Secondary Education Act (ESEA) is being reauthorized. Its largest program, Title I, provides funding to states and districts to improve education for disadvantaged students. However, its funding per student is quite low, averaging about $500 to $600 a year. And there is little evidence that the overall program is effective or that its funds are used for effective services and activities. Large proportions of school principals report using Title I funds for teacher professional development, which many studies have shown to be ineffective and which teachers do not find valuable. Other services on which principals spent Title I funds include after-school and summer programs, technology purchases, and supplemental services, which also have been shown to be ineffective, and class-size reductions, which are unlikely to be of the size needed to generate effects found in previous research.

Achievement gaps between disadvantaged students and their better-off peers are large and have existed for decades. Narrowing these gaps will mean investing more in research to identify effective approaches, or increasing Title I spending by five to eight times more per student, or both. Focusing effective interventions on the neediest students may provide a way forward that is consistent with fiscal realities.

Introduction

Efforts to reauthorize the federal Elementary and Secondary Education Act (ESEA) have generated contentious debates about annual testing and accountability. Both the Senate and House versions, now headed to conference, maintain annual testing and push accountability back to the states. Curiously missing from the debates has been the evidence of whether or not ESEA achieves its objectives.

The largest ESEA expenditure by far is for its Title I program, which in 2014 provided $14 billion to states to improve student achievement. But the last national evaluation that measured Title I's effectiveness, the "Prospects" study, did not find evidence that it improved student achievement.[1] The most recent national assessment of Title I did not measure its effectiveness, though it pointed to broad trends on the National Assessment of Educational Progress showing gains in achievement, especially for minority students. These gains may be due more to NCLB's stricter accountability, however. Accountability created incentives for all public schools to improve.

The question here is whether Title I *funds* are spent effectively.

Follow the Money

Title I has a 60-year history, which is plenty of time for it to develop funding quirks. Funds flow to districts based on their counts of students in poverty, which is determined by the Census Bureau. Districts determine which schools get funds by rank-ordering schools based on poverty levels. Once funds arrive at a school, however, they are used for students at risk of failing to meet state learning standards. A student's poverty level plays no role in determining whether the student is eligible for Title 1 services. And if a school serves at least 40 percent economically disadvantaged students, funds can be used for the entire school (a "schoolwide" program).

There is a well-known correlation between poverty and student achievement, and Title I no doubt serves students who are both poor and underperforming. But the school lunch program does not measure the calorie intake of low-income students and give their lunches away if low-income students are getting "enough" calories. But that is how Title I treats a low-income student who is making satisfactory academic progress.

Title 1 is spread so thin that its budget of $14 billion a year turns out not to be much money.[2] The threshold for operating a Title I schoolwide program is that 40 percent of a school's students are eligible for free or reduced-price lunch, and current data show that 51 percent of students are eligible. Not surprisingly, many schools operate schoolwide programs, in fact about half of all public schools in the United States.[3]

Assuming these schools have average enrollment, which is about 500 students, almost 25 million students attend schools that operate schoolwide programs. The upshot is that after allowing for the money also spent on "targeted-assistance" programs (which operate in schools whose poverty levels are below 40 percent), Title I is spending about $500 to $600 per student. The national assessment of Title 1 used a survey of states, school districts, and schools to estimate Title I expenditures, and essentially reached the same conclusion. Their more exact estimate is that Title I spent $558 per student in a high-poverty school and, another spending quirk, spent $763 per student in a low-poverty school.[4] Education spending was $12,400 a year per student in 2013, which means from the federal perspective, Title I amounts to about 5 percent more per student than would otherwise have been spent.[5]

Realistically, how much improvement can we expect by adding 5 percent to education spending? Data show huge achievement differences for students in poverty compared to those who are not. The National Assessment of Education Progress reported in 2015 that the average fourth grader eligible for free lunch scored 209 in reading, and the average fourth grader that was not eligible for free lunch scored 237. That 28-point gap is roughly comparable to being behind by more than two grade levels. The gap is 25 points in eighth grade, which is still very large.

Spending another $500 seems unlikely to close these kinds of gaps much or at all.

Maybe the funds can be focused on fewer students or spent on highly effective activities or services. But, by design, schoolwide programs do not target specific students. The programs are intended for the whole school, though schools might operate after-school programs or basic skills programs that benefit only those students that attend them. And the question of whether the money is spent effectively is preceded by a question that itself is hard to answer: how *is* the money spent?

What Is Purchased with Title I Funds?

In 2010, the Government Accountability Office visited 12 school districts in four states to explore what happened to the money. The nation's "watchdog" agency could not simply check a database or spreadsheet to determine how Title I money was spent. They had to send investigators into the field. This is not a criticism of the GAO. There is no database they could have referenced, so they went to the field to learn what they could. They did note in their report that Education Department officials "want to allow schools to spend the money to meet their unique needs and to be free to spend the money creatively."

The money might be spent creatively but what the GAO reported is not much cause for thinking the money is spent effectively.[6] Most of the money—84 percent—is spent on "instruction," which is not surprising for a program that operates in schools. Some districts used funds for teacher professional development in the form of workshops or by hiring coaches to support regular classroom teachers, or funded smaller class sizes, provided after-school programs and summer-school programs, or bought technology hardware or software.

These findings are corroborated by recent data from the Early Childhood Longitudinal Study's kindergarten cohort, which administered a survey to principals of schools that included a kindergarten. Principals were asked how they spent Title 1 funds. The survey did not ask dollar amounts or proportions, unfortunately. Principals checked off ways in which money was spent without indicating how much was spent. The table counts principals not receiving Title 1 funds as responding "no spending" in each category.

The table shows that 81 percent of principals reported spending Title I money on professional development. The percent is higher—93 percent—in urban schools and in schools with high poverty rates (more than 75% free or reduced price lunch). How much is spent on professional development is hard to assess because the districts report spending in categories such as "instruction" that includes teachers and teacher aides. If teachers hired through Title I are coaching other teachers, they are counted as teachers and not as professional developers, though that's their role.

What Works and What the Money Is Spent on Are Different Things

Evidence of effectiveness is lacking for nearly all these activities. For example, the New Teacher Project recently reviewed research on the effectiveness of professional development, and the title of its report provides the answer—"The Mirage."[7] They found no evidence of effective professional development programs. They did find evidence of massive expenditures on professional development, even more than in other professional fields, and evidence that teachers mostly disliked professional development activities and did not feel the activities were tailored to their needs.

Two large and rigorous studies of professional development conducted by the Institute of Education Sciences—one focusing on reading[8] and the other on math[9]—likewise found no evidence that intensive professional development improved student achievement. And the professional-development programs the Institute studied were ones that were more expensive and required greater time commitments than ones likely to be supported by Title I.

Other ways in which Title I funds are spent also are not supported by evidence, or are too vaguely reported to know whether they are. After-school programs have been shown not to be effective.[10] The same is true of technology used in classrooms.[11] In the late eighties, a study of class-size reduction in Tennessee showed effects, but to get these effects, class sizes were reduced from an average of 23 students to 15 students. Class-size reductions of this size and expense are not happening in Title I schools based on additional federal funding of a few hundred dollars per student.

Schools in need of improvement also have to use Title I money to support transporting students to schools parents choose, or for supplemental services. The parent choice option was chosen by too few parents to generate much improvement. The national assessment reported that 6 million students were eligible for choice in the 2004-2005 school year and 45,000 used it.[12] And a rigorous study of supplemental services that Mathematica conducted for the Institute of Education Sciences found the services were ineffective.[13]

We Need to Be Realistic or Spend More Wisely

Districts and schools that are recipients of Title I dollars are being asked to tackle disparities of longstanding social and historical origin issues with little money. The program sends token amounts to schools, which use the amounts to funds services that research has found to be ineffective. Educators may appreciate the added resources, but attaching lofty expectations to the resources seems out of touch, as if Washington does not understand that $500 for a student does not go a long way in schools. For comparison, the average public school teacher earns about $50 an hour (the average depends on how fringe benefits are costed).[14] Title 1 spending buys a student about 10 hours a year of a teacher.

It is time to modernize this enterprise. If we want Title I to close achievement gaps, policy needs to provide sufficient funding, clear definitions and metrics for desired outcomes, and better guidance about effective programming, which means continued investments in research to identify effective and ineffective programs. The Senate bill includes language that moves in this direction. It calls for researchers to be on peer-review panels that will assess state plans; for states to review local plans to ensure they are identifying and implementing evidence-based methods and are monitoring and evaluating their implementation, and for local agencies to collect and use data to adjust programs.

It is challenging to put a cost on what it would take to close or even narrow achievement gaps created by poverty. We know $500 won't do it. Researchers in Texas estimated the cost of educating an economically disadvantaged student to reach the same achievement level as other students was 25 percent larger, researchers in Missouri estimated the cost was 56 percent larger, and researchers in New York estimated the cost was 100 percent larger.[15] A recent study that examined education outcomes after court-ordered education spending increases estimated that spending 30 percent more a year on disadvantaged students would add about a year to their education attainment. There are no standard methods and data for estimating added costs of educating disadvantaged students, which contributes to this wide range.

Federal spending does not need to eliminate the gap. K-12 education is primarily a state and local function and will continue to be. A reasonable goal would be to close NAEP score gaps by the equivalent of a year. The wide range of estimates does not provide explicit guidance about how much spending would be needed to reach that objective. Estimates from the study of court-ordered spending suggests it is in the ballpark of about $4,000 a year per student.[16] That's a big increase, and unless Congress wants to spend $100 billion a year on Title 1, the increase needs to be coupled with a focus on fewer students. The newly-authorized program may give districts and schools enhanced flexibility to focus on the neediest students even within schoolwide programs. For example, research is emerging on a highly effective tutoring program that operated within the school day and was supported by Title 1 funds.[17] This kind of program focuses on students that need tutoring. A broader consideration would be to increase the threshold at which a school becomes eligible for a Title 1 schoolwide program. Currently, an *average* school qualifies to be a schoolwide program. Constraining the eligibility rate to be the highest 25 percent of schools in terms of poverty, or even fewer, and using those targeted resources on programs that have been validated with strong research could be a productive way forward that fits within the current fiscal realities of the federal budget.

Endnotes

1. http://files.eric.ed.gov/fulltext/ED413411.pdf
2. In fact, in 2014 the Federal government spent more on school breakfasts and lunches—$16.4 billion—than on Title 1. Spending on school breakfasts and lunches is reported at https://schoolnutrition.org/AboutSchoolMeals/SchoolMealTrendsStats.
3. http://www.southerneducation.org/getattachment/4ac62e27-5260-47a5-9d02-14896ec3a531/A-New-Majority-2015-Update-Low-Income-Students-Now.aspx and https://nces.ed.gov/pubs2012/pesschools10/tables/table_02.asp.
4. http://www2.ed.gov/rschstat/eval/disadv/nclb-targeting/nclb-targeting-highlights.pdf
5. https://nces.ed.gov/fastfacts/display.asp?id=66. Because Title I includes 'targeted' and 'concentration' grants that are intended to focus funds on districts with higher poverty levels, some districts receive more than the national average. For example, the national assessment of Title I reported that East St. Louis—a very poor small city—would receive $1,235 a student and New York City would receive $1,633. However, these higher amounts are offset by districts receiving even lower amounts than the national average.
6. http://www.gao.gov/new.items/d11595.pdf
7. http://tntp.org/assets/documents/TNTP-Mirage_2015.pdf
8. http://ies.ed.gov/ncee/pubs/20084030/
9. http://ies.ed.gov/ncee/pubs/20114024/pdf/20114024.pdf
10. http://www2.ed.gov/rschstat/eval/other/cclcfinalreport/cclcfinal.pdf
11. http://ies.ed.gov/ncee/pdf/20074005.pdf
12. https://www2.ed.gov/rschstat/eval/choice/nclb-choice-ses/highlights.pdf
13. https://ies.ed.gov/ncee/pubs/20124053/pdf/20124053.pdf
14. https://nces.ed.gov/programs/digest/d14/tables/dt14_211.60.asp?current=yes
15. The Texas study can be found at http://bush.tamu.edu/research/faculty/TXSchoolFinance/papers/SchoolOutcomesAndSchoolCosts.pdf, the Missouri study at http://citeseerx.ist.psu.edu/viewdoc/download?doi=10.1.1.219.5238&rep=rep1&type=pdf, the New York study at http://surface.syr.edu/cgi/viewcontent.cgi?article=1102&context=cpr, and the Jackson et al. study of the outcomes of court-ordered spending at http://educationnext.org/boosting-education-attainment-adult-earnings-school-spending.
16. To estimate spending needed to close the gap by the education equivalent of one year, we used Jackson et al.'s finding that increasing per-pupil spending by 10 percent increases education attainment by 0.3 years. The attainment gap is not the same as the score gap, but the cost of closing the score gap has not been studied at the Federal level.
17. http://www.ipr.northwestern.edu/publications/docs/workingpapers/2015/IPR-WP-15-01.pdf

"Children experiencing homelessness
are more likely to experience chronic
diseases, behavioral health concerns,
developmental delays, hunger,
and malnutrition than those who
have homes."

Housing Insecurity Has Lifelong Effects on Children

ECLKC

In the following viewpoint ECLKC explores how homelessness impacts young children. These children are more likely to go hungry, get sick, and have medical and dental health problems. They are also more likely to have long-term mental health challenges due to stress. Government and community intervention can help provide stable housing or address these concerns in other ways. ECLKC is part of Head Start, a government agency that promotes school readiness of children from low-income families.

As you read, consider the following questions:

1. How does this viewpoint define homelessness?
2. What are the major causes of housing insecurity?
3. How can homelessness affect mental health?

"Caring for the Health and Wellness of Children Experiencing Homelessness," ECLKC. Reprinted by permission. https://eclkc.ohs.acf.hhs.gov/publication/caring-health-wellness-children-experiencing-homelessness.

E very year, 1.2 million children under 6 years old experience homelessness in the United States. Many of these children are in early childhood education programs. Explore this tip sheet to learn how homelessness impacts various areas of health and wellness. Discover ways to identify and assess the needs of families experiencing homelessness and connect them to medical and dental homes. Also, find resources and supports to connect families to health and wellness providers.

When working with families experiencing homelessness, it is important to remember that children's health and housing security are closely intertwined. Children experiencing homelessness are more likely to experience chronic diseases, behavioral health concerns, developmental delays, hunger, and malnutrition than those who have homes.

Definition of Homelessness Based on McKinney-Vento

Homelessness refers to a state in which individuals lack a fixed, regular, and adequate nighttime residence, including children who are sharing housing of other persons owing to loss of housing, economic hardship, or similar reason (living in motels, hotels, trailer parks, or camping grounds owing to lack of alternative adequate accommodations; living in emergency or transitional shelters or abandoned in hospitals, cars, parks, public spaces, abandoned buildings, substandard housing, bus or train stations). Homelessness may apply to migrant children under certain circumstances. This document provides information about determining eligibility of McKinney-Vento rights and services.

NOTE: This is a definition used by federal, state, and local educational institutions (e.g., Head Start/Child Care, PART C and Part B).

Causes of Homelessness

Natural disasters (e.g., storms, hurricanes, mudslides, fires) have caused many families to experience homelessness. Domestic violence can also be a reason that families experience homelessness. According to the National Law Center on Homelessness & Poverty, for women, domestic violence is a leading cause of homelessness. The top causes of homelessness among families are lack of affordable housing, unemployment, poverty, and low wages.

Identifying and Assessing Need

1.2 million children under 6 years old in the United States experience homelessness every year. As an early care and education program provider, you may already be serving families with young children who are experiencing homelessness or who are at risk for homelessness. You play an important role in identifying, supporting, and connecting these families to resources that can help keep them healthy. There are many resources to help your program in this process.

Effects of Homelessness on Children's Wealth and Wellness

Children experiencing homelessness may be affected by a variety of health challenges because of difficulty accessing regular health care or not having a medical home, inadequate nutrition and access to food, education interruptions, trauma, and disruption in family dynamics. Children experiencing homelessness are sick at twice the rate of children who have homes. They also go hungry twice as often as children who have homes. Children experiencing homelessness have twice the rate of learning disabilities and three times the rate of emotional and behavioral problems of children who have homes.

Medical and Dental Homes

A medical home plays an important role in supporting children's mental wellness. Encourage families to share updates with a trusted provider in their medical home or help connect them to a medical home if they do not have one. A medical or dental home is not a building or a place. It is an approach to providing comprehensive and high-quality primary care that facilitates partnerships between patients, clinicians, medical or dental staff, and families. A medical or dental home extends beyond the four walls of a clinical practice. It includes specialty care, educational services, family support, and more. A key strategy to improving the health and wellness of families experiencing homelessness is to connect them to medical and dental homes. Early care and education programs can play an important role in connecting families experiencing homelessness to medical and dental homes that provide comprehensive and coordinated services that can help address their ongoing health concerns and special health care needs and provide stability and consistency in care that is often missing for these families.

Mental Health and Families Experiencing Homelessness

Recent studies on adverse childhood experiences have shown that multiple stressors that begin in childhood can have long-term adverse effects on a child's neurobiological make-up, cognitive ability, and mental health, as well as on their ability to manage stressors as an adult. Studies also show that these effects can lead to chronic physical health problems. Adults experiencing homelessness have higher levels of stress and depression than those who have homes, which can make parenting young children difficult. Therefore, it is very important to address mental wellness and identify mental health resources and services for families experiencing homelessness. Your program may have access to mental health consultants who can help you develop strategies to support resilience in families experiencing homelessness.

Oral Health and Homelessness

Children experiencing homelessness are less likely to visit a dentist than children from families with low incomes who have homes. Families experiencing homelessness may find it difficult to carry belongings, including a toothbrush and toothpaste. They may have limited access to facilities where they can brush their teeth. Most children experiencing homelessness are eligible for oral health services paid for by Medicaid. However, outreach efforts are not adequate to reach many of these families. The key to supporting the oral health of families experiencing homelessness is to assist them with accessing services to help maintain healthy habits like toothbrushing with fluoride toothpaste and drinking water. Your program may also want to partner with local homeless shelters

CHALLENGES FOR HOMELESS STUDENTS

For a student experiencing homelessness, who the night before was rushing to get across town to get to a shelter before all the beds are full, getting to class the next day and staying awake during class would be a challenge. Often homeless youth change schools so frequently that it impacts their ability to achieve a quality education.

School breaks for many homeless youth are a period of uncertainty and stress. For some youth, school is a place to go for a few hours that is sure to be more peaceful than the streets. Yet during school breaks, youth can be put in a very tough situation. For some youth, what should be a leisurely break quickly becomes one of stress and fear. While many of their classmates are home on break, many homeless youth are looking for a safe place to sleep, childcare, employment, and a meal.

Young people experiencing homelessness also face challenges while accessing housing services, particularly at adult shelters. They sometimes avoid going to adult shelters because they contain the many vices homeless youth try to avoid: drugs, alcohol, violence, fighting, and even sexual assault.

"Youth Experiencing Homelessness Face Many Challenges," SAMHSA, December 8, 2019.

and health and wellness partners to provide services in-house to families.

When Working with Children Who Are Homeless It Is Important to Keep in Mind the Following

Regulations/Funding: Become familiar with regulations that provide flexibility or grace periods related to completing paperwork and meeting health requirement deadlines for families experiencing homelessness.

Social Services: Identify and connect with social service programs that can assist with obtaining stable housing or safe temporary housing and emergency funds for rent, utilities, and support services.

Cultural Perspectives: When working with families experiencing homelessness, use strengths-based approaches that include perspectives of different cultures.

Partnerships: Connect with community health and wellness partners to maintain and promote healthy environments for children (e.g., park districts, museums, boy's and girl's clubs).

Physical Health

- Determine eligibility and help families enroll in Medicaid or other health insurance.
- Work with families to identify or maintain connections to medical and dental homes where they feel supported.
- Help families access high quality mental health, oral health, and physical health services.
- Promote ongoing well child care visits, including health and developmental screenings and preventive care with the same providers at medical and dental homes.
- Promote continuous, ongoing physical health and oral health visits for sick child care at a consistent location where medical and dental history is easy to access (medical or dental home).

Nutrition/Healthy Active Living

- Homeless shelters often provide foods that lack adequate nutrients for infants, toddlers, and preschool children and instead provide foods high in fat and low in fiber.
- Connect with food and nutrition assistance programs such as WIC to secure access to healthy foods for families experiencing homelessness.
- Work with families on simple strategies to keep children active.

Mental Health

- Support the social-emotional health of infants, toddlers, and preschool children by utilizing mental health consultants.
- Explore training opportunities on trauma-informed practices to support children and families experiencing homelessness.
- Connect with mental health centers or medical homes with behavioral health specialists to assess children's and families' mental health needs during transitions into homelessness.

Parent and Family Supports

- Work with parenting supports or home visiting programs to help identify strategies to create healthy activities for parents experiencing homelessness.
- Become familiar with resources available to help prevent families from experiencing homelessness.
- Work collaboratively with families experiencing homelessness to help them access resources.
- Become familiar with resources available to families with young children experiencing homelessness.
- Develop strong relationships with families experiencing homelessness to help build resilience and trust.

> *"Out-of-school experiences offer important ways for students to develop academic skills like critical thinking and problem-solving, as well as social-emotional skills such as persistence and teamwork."*

Family Wealth Affects Out of School Opportunities

Ashley Jochim

In the following excerpted viewpoint Ashley Jochim compares two fictional students. One student receives a great deal of support from her family and school, while the other student does not. This disparity leads to a description of how parental wealth affects the opportunities that school-age children have. For instance, the children of wealthy parents are much more likely to participate in a variety of educational activities outside of school. This further widens the gap between them and students from low-income families. The author argues that to achieve equity, or even equality, this difference in opportunity must be addressed. Ashley Jochim is a senior research analyst at the Center on Reinventing Public Education.

"Analysis—We Need a New Way to Talk About Educational Equity: From Achievement Gaps to Out-of-School Enrichment, Postsecondary Preparation and Beyond," by Ashley Jochim, The 74, March 18, 2019. Reprinted by permission.

As you read, consider the following questions:

1. Is equality in education getting better or worse, according to the viewpoint?
2. What are some out of school activities more available to children of wealthy parents?
3. How does the situation described affect students with disabilities?

Ally and Stacy are typical American high school seniors. Ally leaves her Advanced Placement American government class feeling excited after a stimulating debate over the merits of free speech. After school, she attends her student government club and then meets with her tutor, who is helping her prepare for the SAT. That evening, after completing the work associated with an online college course that she enrolled in, Ally and her parents discuss plans for summer, which include an internship with a local business and a two-week camp for aspiring leaders. She's looking forward to graduation and feels good about where she's headed after consulting with her private college advisor, who helped the family wade through the many options.

Stacy is not so lucky. She leaves her remedial math class feeling bored and defeated—hardly surprising after spending the last 30 minutes working through an online module meant to catch her up. She doesn't have anywhere to go after school, so she heads to the local park with friends. Summer's just around the corner, but she's not looking forward to it. If she doesn't pass her math class, she'll have to go to summer school, otherwise known as "purgatory" to the students who attend. She's worried about what she's going to do after graduation, but the school's guidance counselor is only available once a week and it's impossible to get an appointment.

Ally's and Stacy's stories are typical. They play out all over the United States every day, sometimes even in the same school, and reveal a lot about the growth in educational inequality over the last half century. One student enjoys challenging coursework in school, a wealth of enrichment opportunities outside of school, and a support system, including college-educated parents, that helps her prepare for post-secondary opportunities. The other languishes with disengaging coursework designed to fill academic gaps that emerged years earlier, a dearth of enrichment opportunities, and limited access to guidance or other resources that might allow her to improve her situation—much less pursue a postsecondary education that would allow her to maximize her potential.

For much of American history, public education has been cherished as the engine of upward mobility even as it struggled to deliver on the promise of equal opportunity. While progress has been made, opportunities for public education to bridge the gaps between students and families of different circumstances remain severely compromised and may be getting worse.

Addressing all of the sources of educational inequality illustrated by students like Ally and Stacy will require a broader perspective, widening the lens beyond an exclusive focus on the historical issues of funding, segregation, and the achievement gap. This essay considers the changes in American education that are upending traditional notions of equity in education and offers ideas on how policymakers could act to address this issue in the future.

New Challenges to Equity in Education

Expanding access to educational opportunity has defined debates over school reform for nearly a century, including desegregation efforts, finance equalization cases, and proposals to expand school choice. Despite notable progress in some areas, opportunity is more stratified than ever along the lines of race and class.

While the issues of racial and income-based segregation, inadequate spending, and gaps in achievement continue to define educational inequality, they fail to capture broader societal shifts that are changing the ways we think about youth development. These include increased household spending on out-of-school learning experiences, particularly among wealthy families; the growing complexity of postsecondary educational opportunities;

and the importance of non-achievement-based educational outcomes. These shifts highlight sources of educational inequality that, to date, policy has largely failed to address—and at times actively undermined—and suggest new ways for improving opportunity for America's most vulnerable children.

The Growth in Out-of-School Learning Experiences

Two decades of school reform have sought to address educational inequality by "fixing" schools. And yet, students increasingly don't rely on traditional K–12 schools to prepare them for success in life. Wealthy families are investing growing amounts of time and money into the education of their children, a phenomenon Garey and Valerie Ramey deem "the rug rat race." While all families spend more time with their children than in decades past, college-educated parents have made pronounced investments in providing enriching out-of-school experiences for their children. According to a 2015 survey conducted by the Pew Research Center, children of wealthy parents are substantially more likely to have participated in sports, done volunteer work, taken music, dance, or art lessons, and participated in religious instruction or youth groups. Just 7 percent of low-income children attend summer camp, compared to nearly 40 percent of high-income children. The gap between wealthy and poor families' expenditures on enrichment activities more than doubled between the 1970s and the mid-2000s.

These challenges don't just mean fewer "fun" experiences for low-income children. Out-of-school experiences offer important ways for students to develop academic skills like critical thinking and problem-solving, as well as social-emotional skills such as persistence and teamwork. These experiences may be especially important for low-income students and students of color, who are less likely to have access to teachers and curricula that develop these skills in school.

The lack of enrichment compounds the disadvantages these students face as it relates to access to other resources that support readiness to learn. Too many students enter the classroom with challenges that cannot be resolved by schools alone, including exposure to trauma and unaddressed basic health care needs. To date, policymakers and educators have sought to address these challenges by investing in wraparound services, which offer a continuum of care within the walls of the school. But such models have proven expensive to deliver and difficult to coordinate, and leave little room for families to customize supports to address their unique needs.

While most considerations of inequality in education focus on low-income students and students of color, students with disabilities also have been profoundly affected by the growth of out-of-school learning experiences. Consider, for example, the search for afterschool programs and summer camps for a student with autism. The private organizations that offer such programs are even less equipped than public schools to make accommodations for students with a disability. The most advantaged parents can rely on their social networks and wallets to secure a meaningful set of experiences for their children. But low-income students and students of color are disproportionately represented among students with disabilities, and are less likely to have access to the resources that would enable them to tap into those experiences.

[…]

Conclusion

To be sure, none of these investments are a substitute for strong classroom-based instruction. There is much to be gained from continued work to improve public schools as they currently exist, while they continue to face challenges related to underinvestment, shortages of teacher talent, and weaknesses in curriculum and instructional support.

But a vision for educational equality must address all of the factors that shape students' educational experiences—including access to out-of-school enrichment, preparation for postsecondary education, and domains of learning that are not captured by traditional achievement measures but may be crucial to allowing students to succeed in 21st century learning environments. Wealthy families increasingly use the resources at their disposal to provide these experiences for their children. A truly equitable public education system would ensure these experiences are equally available to everyone, and allow disadvantaged families to exercise the same levels of choice and agency as their more advantaged counterparts.

If people who care about public education do not open themselves up to new ways to address inequality, not only will they give up the chance to break through the political deadlock that has characterized school reform fights, but they also are unlikely to make headway in equalizing opportunity for American students.

"Attracting teachers to poor, remote communities exacerbates teacher shortages, because the pay is often low and there's higher turnover."

Rural Schools Have Their Own Challenges

Liz Teitz

In the following viewpoint Liz Teitz explores issues surrounding rural schools. These schools face many significant challenges. For one, it can be harder to hire qualified teachers at these schools. Rural schools may lack resources available in cities. State and federal policies may not work well in rural areas. Rural schools can succeed, the author writes, and so can the students in them, but the schools must be able to address problems in a way appropriate for their situation. Liz Teitz is a reporter who covers higher education and politics.

As you read, consider the following questions:

1. How many students nationwide attend rural schools?
2. Why do rural school sometimes find it hard to get exceptional teachers?
3. Why is school district consolidation often a problem for rural schools, according to the viewpoint?

R ural schools often get short shrift in the national dialogue on improving education and addressing achievement gaps, whether it's policy debates, research, or news coverage. That's a big mistake, according to participants in a recent EWA panel discussion, who made the case for reporters to pay more attention to education in rural communities.

Along the way, the speakers dispensed plenty of advice and story angles. That includes examining the challenge of recruiting qualified teachers to rural areas, spotlighting funding disparities, and looking at how federal and state mandates sometimes are ill-suited to rural settings. Another theme? Don't pigeonhole rural communities.

Nationally, nearly nine million students attend rural schools, which is more than the number of students in New York City, Chicago, Los Angeles and the next 75 largest school districts combined, said Alan Richard, chairman of The Rural School and Community Trust.

He emphasized that there are "many faces" of rural students in America. "Rural in New England looks a little different than the Mississippi Delta or rural California or Indian Country," Richard said.

Half of the nation's rural students live in 10 states, according to Richard, many of which aren't states commonly thought of as "rural," such as Ohio, New York, and Pennsylvania.

Teacher Shortages

Reporter Noel Gallagher of the Portland Press-Herald in Maine described vast disparities in that state between wealthy coastal communities, "husks of cities around empty mills" and remote towns. The challenges faced by schools across the country are made more acute in rural areas, she said. Attracting teachers to poor, remote communities exacerbates teacher shortages, because the pay is often low and there's higher turnover, she said.

In the classroom, rural students often have access to fewer educational opportunities than suburban and urban peers, such as access to Advanced Placement classes, according to Gallagher. When reporting on rural education, she said it's important to spend time in the communities to understand the unique issues and assets they're covering.

"Get there on the ground," she said. "That will inform your reporting more than anything."

Also, journalists should incorporate the voices of rural communities and address the advantages and innovations in rural schools, not just the problems, speakers said.

"Every situation is not completely dire," said Richard of The Rural Schools and Communities Trust. "Every story that's about rural doesn't have to be a rural story."

Voices from those communities should be included in broader stories about trends, state policies or school funding, he suggested.

State and Federal Mandates

Another speaker, Campbell Scribner, an assistant professor of education at the University of Maryland, said that more attention should be paid to closing achievement gaps in rural education. Journalists also should be aware of disconnects between the needs of rural schools and state and federal mandates, he said.

Some state and federal policies "patently cannot work in rural areas," Scribner said. He cited examples under the federal No Child Left Behind Act that gave exceptions to rural school districts that could not meet requirements for "highly qualified" teachers. Oftentimes, teachers in small rural districts might teach multiple subjects. (NCLB was replaced in 2015 by the Every Student Succeeds Act.)

Richard called the lack of resources in many rural schools an emergency. He added that school district consolidation, which is often floated as a solution, doesn't necessarily save districts much money. Also, it may cause more problems for staff and students when it creates districts across far-flung communities.

In Maine, schools in communities that have been devastated by economic downturns "are under tremendous pressure to consolidate and save money," Gallagher said. But when schools are the heart of a community, and when districts are far apart from each other, consolidation isn't necessarily the answer.

New problems can arise: transportation times may increase and poor communities can be forced to take on a higher tax burden, she said. And while the trend toward combining districts has slowed in some areas, reporters should be aware of it happening under other names.

In Maine, the school funding formula penalizes districts that don't consolidate, which is hardest for schools that are more geographically remote, Gallagher said. Because they'll lose funding if they don't find ways to share scarce resources, districts are looking at ways to regionalize certain departments, such as payroll, she said.

In situations where consolidation is necessary, such as due to a dwindling population, "the community is best at making decisions for itself," Richard said. "What hasn't been so successful are state-imposed consolidations."

In some cases, the benefits of rural schools are being rediscovered elsewhere and can offer a model for all schools, Scribner said. He pointed to the development of small schools and schools-within-schools, which mirror realities in rural education where it's just "common sense."

Conversations about hands-on, experiential learning are also already taking place in rural communities, where links between the classroom and life outside are made obvious.

"They're able to walk out the front doors and have parents and teachers teaching them about local economies," which also sets up opportunities for mentoring and bringing parents into the classroom, Gallagher said.

Periodical and Internet Sources Bibliography

The following articles have been selected to supplement the diverse views presented in this chapter.

FastBridge, "Educational Equity for Children in Poverty," January 4, 2019. https://www.fastbridge.org/2019/01/educational-equity -children-poverty/

Institute for Children, Poverty & Homelessness, "Addressing Barriers to Learning," https://www.icphusa.org/reports/addressing -barriers-to-learning/#overview

Derrick Meador, "How the Federal Title I Program Helps Students and Schools," Thought Co., July 03, 2019. https://www.thoughtco .com/how-the-federal-title-i-program-helps-students-and -schools-3194750

William Parrett and Kathleen Budge, "How Does Poverty Influence Learning?" Edutopia, January 13, 2016. https://www.edutopia .org/blog/how-does-poverty-influence-learning-william-parrett -kathleen-budge

Emily Richmond, "Why It's Time to Focus on Equity in Rural Schools," Education Writers Association, January 24, 2019. https://www.ewa.org/blog-educated-reporter/why-its-time-focus -equity-rural-schools

Substance Abuse and Mental Health Services Administration, "Youth Experiencing Homelessness Face Many Challenges," December 08, 2019. https://www.samhsa.gov/homelessness-programs -resources/hpr-resources/youth-experiencing-homelessness

Heather Biggar Tomlinson, "Gaining Ground on Equity for Rural Schools and Communities," Mid-Atlantic Equity Consortium, September 2020. https://maec.org/resource/gaining-ground-on -equity-for-rural-schools-and-communities/

Sara Wolforth and Julie Kochanek, "Addressing Challenges and Elevating Opportunities in Rural Education," American Institutes for Research, https://www.air.org/resource/addressing -challenges-and-elevating-opportunities-rural-education

OPPOSING
VIEWPOINTS®
SERIES

CHAPTER 5

How Can Educational Equity Be Achieved?

Chapter Preface

The previous chapters have attempted to explain equality versus equity in education. They have also made a case for the value of equity in education while recognizing the challenges. That leads to the question of how equity in education can be achieved. Education experts have several ideas.

Personalized learning provides each student with an individualized program. Instead of giving every student the same lesson and the same tests, each student works independently. They still need to learn the same skills, but they can learn based on their strengths, needs, and interests.

Community schools recognize that students may need help outside of school as well as in school. These schools partner with community agencies to provide a variety of services. Services may include healthcare, dental care, counseling, extended learning time, and tutoring. Community schools may even provide legal help and transportation. These schools can keep students happier and help more of them graduate. Community schools work with parents and other community members as well, building a healthier community.

Personalized learning and community schools are challenging to implement. They require major changes, including teacher training. Some programs designed to build equity in education can be done more on a departmental or classroom basis. Standards-based learning puts less emphasis on grades. Teachers and administrators try to help students with any behavioral problems separately. For example if a student turns in a paper late, that doesn't affect their grade.

Systemic racism remains a problem in schools. Culturally responsive teaching attempts to challenge the traditions that center white history and values. It engages and respects students from all races and cultures.

Disciplinary policies are often racist and unsuccessful. Practices such as suspension and expulsion help neither the student nor the school as a whole. Antiracism training can help root out unconscious bias in teachers and the administration. Some schools are exploring alternatives that support students who are in trouble rather than simply punishing them.

The American dream promises equal opportunity for everyone. The educational system has failed to support that dream. Redesigning schools to support equity in education may help more people reach the American dream. This chapter explores several options for attaining this.

| "Kids learn in different ways and at different paces. Personalized learning is a teaching model based on that premise."

Personalized Learning Paths Allow for Student Differences

Amanda Morin

In the following viewpoint, Amanda Morin explains the concept of personalized learning. This style of education attempts to give each student an individualized learning program that is appropriate for that child. Teachers monitor the students to make sure they stay on track. Personalized learning is not widely used, but advocates say it offers advantages. In order to expand programs such as these, teachers will have to be properly trained. Amanda Morin is an author and former early childhood educator.

As you read, consider the following questions:

1. According to the viewpoint, is personalized learning a type of special education?
2. What is a "modality" in personalized learning?
3. What is the advantage of personalized learning over IEPs, according to the author?

To get an idea of what personalized learning is, try to picture a classroom that doesn't have a "one size fits all" approach to education. The teacher doesn't lead all students through the same lessons. Instead, the teacher guides each student on an individualized journey. The what, when, where and how of learning is tailored to meet each student's strengths , skills, needs, and interests.

Students may learn some skills at different paces. But their learning plans still keep them on track to meet the standards for a high school diploma.

That kind of classroom isn't the reality for most students. But it's the end goal of personalized learning, which is already being used successfully in some schools and is expanding in several states. Here's what you need to know.

What Personalized Learning Is

Kids learn in different ways and at different paces. Personalized learning is a teaching model based on that premise. Each student gets a "learning plan" based on how they learn, what they know, and what their skills and interests are. It's the opposite of the "one size fits all" approach used in most schools.

Students work with their teachers to set both short-term and long-term goals. This process helps students take ownership of their learning.

Teachers make sure learning plans or project-based learning match up with academic standards. And they check to see if students are demonstrating the skills they're expected to learn as they progress through their education.

Personalized learning is not a replacement for special education. It's an approach to general education that can work with an Individualized Education Program (IEP), a 504 plan , response to intervention, or other specialized intervention programs.

But accommodations, supports, and accessible learning strategies need to be essential parts of personalized learning. If done well, all students will be more engaged in their learning. And struggling students will get help sooner. If not done well, students with disabilities could fall further behind.

How Personalized Learning Works

No two schools using personalized learning will look exactly the same. But here are four widely used models that schools follow. Each of these models sets high expectations for all students and aligns their learning to a set of rigorous standards.

1. Schools That Use Learner Profiles

This type of school keeps an up-to-date record that provides a deep understanding of each student's individual strengths, needs, motivations, progress and goals. These profiles are updated far more often than a standard report card. And these detailed updates help teachers make decisions to positively impact student learning.

A learner profile also helps students keep track of their own progress. It gives the teacher, the student and, in many schools, the parent a way to know if they need to change a learning method or make changes to goals—before the student does poorly or fails.

2. Schools That Use Personalized Learning Paths

This type of school helps each student customize a learning path that responds or adapts based on progress, motivations, and goals. For instance, a school might create a student's schedule based on weekly updates about academic progress and interests.

Each student's schedule is unique. But it's likely to include several learning methods. (These are often called modalities.) The mix might include project-based learning with a small group of peers, independent work on certain skills or complex tasks, and one-on-one tutoring with a teacher.

A personalized learning path allows a student to work on different skills at different paces. But that doesn't mean the school will let a student fall far behind in any area. Teachers closely monitor each student and provide extra support as needed.

3. Schools That Use Competency-Based Progression

This type of school continually assesses students to monitor their progress toward specific goals. This system makes it clear to students what they need to master. These competencies include specific skills, knowledge and mindsets like developing resilience.

Students are given options of how and when to demonstrate their mastery. For example, a student might work with a teacher to weave certain math skills into an internship at a retail store.

The student might work on several competencies at the same time. When they master one, they move on to the next. Each student gets the necessary support or services to help master the skills. The emphasis isn't on taking a test and getting a passing or failing grade. Instead, it's about continuous learning and having many chances to show knowledge.

4. Schools Using Flexible Learning Environments

This type of school adapts the environment students learn in, based on how they learn best. That includes things like the physical setup of the class, how the school day is structured and how the teachers are allocated.

For example, schools might look for ways to give teachers more time for small group instruction. It's not easy to redesign the way teachers use space, time and resources in the classroom. But this type of design thinking can help student needs reshape the learning environment.

The Potential of Personalized Learning

Personalized learning isn't widely used in schools yet. Many aspects still need to be explored. But this approach has the potential to help reduce the stigma of special education and better meet the needs of kids with learning and thinking differences.

IEPs are too often focused mainly on deficits. But personalized learning paths can balance that by focusing on students' strengths and interests. Together, IEPs and personalized learning can give kids the supports to work on weaknesses and a customized path that engages their interests and helps them "own" their learning.

Personalized learning can also give students the chance to build self-advocacy skills . It encourages them to speak up about what interests them. It also allows them to be equal partners in their learning experience.

Personalized learning has a lot of potential, but it also has some risks. Teachers might not have enough inclusion training to make this approach accessible to all students. They might not know how to support kids with executive functioning issues . They might not know how to track competencies or analyze other kinds of student data.

The key is to make sure that when schools start using personalized learning, teachers have the training to meet your child's needs. And the more you know, the more involved you can be in the conversation.

> "This way, students can see themselves
> in some of what they're reading and
> not just the white, western world."

Culturally Responsive Teaching
Is for Everyone

Kristin Burnham

In the following viewpoint Kristin Burnham explains culturally responsive teaching. This style of teaching attempts to recognize the importance of students' varied cultures and how that affects learning. This differs from traditional teaching, which tends to center on white history and treat the teacher as the expert passing on information in one direction. Culturally responsive teaching recognizes that every culture has value and that in some cases, students may be more expert than teachers. Culturally responsive teaching can help students feel more respected and engaged. Kristin Burnham is a reporter and editor.

As you read, consider the following questions:

1. Is culturally responsive teaching only relevant for certain students?
2. How can culturally responsive teaching make students feel valued, according to the viewpoint?
3. What cultures and backgrounds can be supported by culturally responsive teaching?

"5 Culturally Responsive Teaching Strategies," by Kristin Burnham, Northeastern University, July 31, 2020. Reprinted by permission.

Over the past few decades, students, their experiences, upbringings, and backgrounds have changed. Classrooms now reflect families of varying races, cultures, and socioeconomic statuses. As a result, the way teachers educate these students must change, too, says Cherese Childers-Mckee, assistant teaching professor in Northeastern University's College of Professional Studies. One of these shifting approaches to education is known as culturally responsive teaching.

Below, we explore the concept of culturally responsive teaching, compare it against traditional teaching models, and offer a number of strategies that you can use to incorporate the approach into your own methods.

What Is Culturally Responsive Teaching?

Culturally responsive teaching, also called culturally relevant teaching, is a pedagogy that recognizes the importance of including students' cultural references in all aspects of learning. Traditional teaching strategies emphasize the teacher-student dynamic: The teacher is the expert and adheres strictly to the curriculum that supports standardized tests while the student receives the knowledge. This teaching method is outdated, Childers-Mckee says.

"Teachers have more diverse classrooms today. We don't have students sitting in front of us with the same background or experience, so instruction has to be different," she says. "It needs to build on individual and cultural experiences and their prior knowledge. It needs to be justice-oriented and reflect the social context we're in now. That's what we mean when we talk about culturally responsive teaching."

Culturally Responsive vs. Traditional Teaching Methods

Culturally responsive teaching can manifest in a number of ways. Using traditional teaching methods, educators may default to teaching literature by widely accepted classic authors: William

Shakespeare, J.D. Salinger, and Charles Dickens, for example, adhering to widely accepted interpretations of the text.

Culturally responsive teaching, on the other hand, acknowledges that there's nothing wrong with traditional texts, Childers-McKee says, but strives to include literature from other cultures, parts of the world, and by diverse authors. It also focuses on finding a "hook and anchor" to help draw students into the content using their past experiences.

"This way, students can see themselves in some of what they're reading and not just the white, western world. The learning is more experimental, more hands-on," she says. "Instead, you're showing them a worldwide, multicultural community and looking for different interpretations while relating it to what it means for society today."

Why Is Culturally Responsive Teaching Important?

Culturally responsive teaching is especially pertinent today because the traditional education path from school to college to a career and life in the suburbs isn't a reality—or desire—for everyone, Childers-McKee says. Educators' approaches to teaching need to reflect these differences.

"That typical, mainstream education is not addressing the realities of today's students. Culturally responsive teaching isn't just for those students who don't come from white, middle-class, English-speaking families—it's an important teaching strategy for everyone. When done the right way, it can be transformative."

When integrated into classroom instruction, culturally responsive strategies can have important benefits such as:

- Strengthening students' sense of identity
- Promoting equity and inclusivity in the classroom
- Engaging students in the course material
- Supporting critical thinking

Here's a look at five culturally responsive teaching strategies all educators can employ in their classrooms.

5 Culturally Responsive Teaching Strategies for Educators

1. Activate Students' Prior Knowledge

Students are not blank slates, Childers-McKee says; they enter the classroom with diverse experiences. Teachers should encourage students to draw on their prior knowledge in order to contribute to group discussions, which provides an anchor to learning. Taking a different approach to the literature that's taught in classrooms is one example of this.

2. Make Learning Contextual

Tie lessons from the curriculum to the students' social communities to make it more contextual and relevant, Childers-McKee advises. "If you're reading a chapter in history class, for example, discuss why it matters today, in your school, or in your community," she says. "Take the concept you're learning about and create a project that enables them to draw parallels."

3. Encourage Students to Leverage Their Cultural Capital

Because not all students come from the same background, it's important to encourage those who don't to have a voice. Say, for example, you teach an English class that contains ESL students. It's important to find ways to activate the experiences they do have—their cultural capital, Childers-McKee says.

The teacher may choose a book for the class to read in which the ESL students could relate and feel like they could be the expert, for instance. As a teacher, Childers-Mckee's once chose a book that told the story of a child of migrant workers because some of her students came from an agricultural background.

"When you have a mixed classroom, you want those in the minority to feel like they are an expert. You want to draw from their experiences," she says. "I do caution that you don't want to cross a line and make 'Johnny' feel like he needs to speak for all Mexican people by putting them on the spot, for example. That's a line you need to walk."

Implicit Bias and Cultural Sensitivity Training

Left unchecked, implicit bias contributes to cultural insensitivity, which creates barriers to inclusion, performance, and engagement. To interrupt the impact of unfavorable implicit bias on learning outcomes, school leaders need to leverage training that supports teachers in exploring the following: * Individual biases and how to adjust them * Benefits of cultural sensitivity and culturally responsive pedagogy * Negative implications associated with ignoring implicit bias * How schools address implicit bias in decision-making and pedagogy Cultural sensitivity precedes culturally responsive pedagogy, and implicit bias training supports development of cultural sensitivity. Benefits of culturally responsive pedagogy include positive effects on teacher expectations, student achievement, cross-cultural communications, and the design of learning experiences. School leaders who leverage implicit bias training to promote cultural sensitivity understand that effective teaching is culturally responsive.

Prioritizing implicit bias training to ensure cultural sensitivity supports teachers in responding positively and constructively to diverse students. After completing implicit bias training, teachers are more prone to engage in ongoing self-reflection and analysis of underlying assumptions. Through these practices, teachers gain greater self-awareness of implicit biases, develop greater cultural sensitivity, and understand the importance of implementing culturally responsive pedagogy for the success of all students.

"Implicit Bias and Cultural Sensitivity Training," Future Ready Schools.

4. Reconsider Your Classroom Setup

Take inventory of the books in your classroom library: Do they include authors of diverse races? Is the LGB community represented? Do the books include urban families or only suburban families? Beyond your classroom library, consider the posters you display on your walls and your bulletin boards, too. "These are all small changes you can make to your classroom more culturally responsive," Childers-McKee says.

5. Build Relationships

Not all students want to learn from all teachers because the teachers may not make them feel like they're valued, Childers-McKee says. Teachers need to work to build relationships with their students to ensure they feel respected, valued, and seen for who they are. Building those relationships helps them build community within the classroom and with each other, which is extremely important, she says.

"When we think about culture and diversity, people often automatically think about black students, but people need to think broader than that, now," Childers-McKee says. "Some teachers whose students are all white and middle-class struggle with how culturally responsive teaching strategies apply to them. It's equally important for them to teach students about diversity. These aren't just teaching strategies for minorities, they're good teaching strategies for everyone."

> *"So when asking, 'Why the change to standards-based grading?' Consider if what you are doing is not working and leaving you dissatisfied."*

Switch to Standards-Based Learning

Karen Hernandez

In the following viewpoint Karen Hernandez explains why she and her department decided to switch to standards-based teaching. This teaching method claims traditional grading practices aren't working. Instead, student behavior, such as turning in assignments late, should not result in lower grades. Academic achievement should be separate from behavior, and students should get support in order to make improvements in any areas where they show weakness. Karen Hernandez is a high school math teacher and department head in California.

As you read, consider the following questions:

1. According to the author, why does standards-based teaching separate academics from behavior?
2. What advantages does standards-based teaching have for students?
3. Why might it be hard for teachers or schools to switch to standards-based grading?

As the chair of the math department at my high school, I am always looking for ways to support our teachers and students. Whether I'm sharing an instructional strategy or a new pedagogical point of view, my goal is always to work collaboratively with teachers for our shared purpose: supporting our students. Last year, I found myself constantly questioning if the way I assessed and graded students accurately reflected their level of proficiency, and if the feedback I provided was enough to help them improve. I wondered if teachers in my department felt similarly. It turns out they did, and these uncertainties (and our desire to feel more confident in our instruction) are what led my content team to standards-based teaching.

Making the transition from traditional grading to standards-based teaching and grading was exciting and intimidating because I did not know where to start or how to go about it but I knew it was necessary. In this blog post, I'll discuss the inspiration behind the change, an example of what the changeover looked like, and our implementation of standards-based feedback.

Inspiration

After attending several conferences centered on collaborative common assessments, I was introduced to the book Standards-Based Learning in Action. This book was exactly what my team needed to make our switch. The book is designed to guide teachers on breaking down the current traditional grading practices happening in the classroom, why they aren't working, and why standards-based teaching and learning will support instruction better. Throughout the reading, I reflected on how I could shift my teaching and grading practices to best serve the needs of my students.

The four core principles that the team took away from the book were: 1) separating behavioral factors from the academic grade, 2) how to create formative and summative assessments, 3) how to give feedback, and 4) how to actively use feedback for student improvement. Personally, I found the feedback chapter–and using it for student improvement–to be the most empowering areas of reading and the most exciting to implement.

Changeover

Let's take a look at the core principle of separating behavioral factors from the academic grades. As an example, if a student turned in an assignment late, I used to give him/her half credit. Why? It was the norm I learned when I started teaching. However, what if the work was completely accurate and the only problem was punctuality? Should a student's grade be affected? No. The timeliness of work submission is what requires attention–as well as solutions to such an issue–not the grade. This falls under behavioral characteristics, or separating the academics from behavior. With standards-based teaching and grading we can focus on the three important factors: standard(s) proficiency, behavior, and academic growth. This focus results in what all teachers want: students performing to their best abilities.

Now that we've seen a separation of academic and behavioral grading, let's look at how to create academic growth with standards-based feedback. With grades, how many of us can relate to using the percentage breakdown 20% Homework, 30% Tests, 10% Participation, 40% Final Exam, or something similar? I know I used to. But where in these four categories do we capture the skill(s)/standard(s) where students need support? Truthfully, we can't do that with this breakdown model. This picture does not give an adequate breakdown of students' academic performance on the standards and mastery of them. With standards-based reflection, you get a clear snapshot of students' strengths and areas for growth within the standards. It is evident if the student is weak in one standard but stronger in a related standard, giving me an area to focus on for remediations.

Initial Implementation

Over the course of time, our team, with administration support, actively moved through implementing the core principles. Our transition had its challenges, from finding the time to do the work to learning how to collaborate frequently on creating collaborative common assessments. Our first action step was to rearrange our curriculum modules so as to align with the last unit from eighth grade and end with a transitional unit into Integrated Math II. This alignment helps students see the connections between the transition of the math content from middle school to high school. For teachers, it helps them visually see the cohesiveness of the standards within the modules for all three grade levels. Our next action step focused on selecting essential standards necessary for Integrated Math 1 based on the vertical articulation of our standards between Integrated Math 1 through Integrated Math II. Finally, our third step centered on the development of each unit and how to give the best first instruction.

In conclusion, although this transition may sound tedious and/or time consuming (at times it may be), think of it as "you have to go slow to go fast." So when asking, "Why the change to standards-based grading?" Consider if what you are doing is not working and leaving you dissatisfied. If so, then why not?

> *"Suspensions have been correlated to poor student outcomes, including decreased student achievement, lower graduation rates, higher dropout rates, suppressed student engagement, and future disciplinary exclusion."*

Rethink School Discipline

David Hinojosa

In the following viewpoint David Hinojosa considers disciplinary practices in education. Traditional disciplinary policies are often ineffective and unfair, Hinojosa argues. They disproportionately affect students of color, likely due to educators' subconscious racial bias. Teachers can try to overcome their subconscious bias, but student discipline must also be addressed at the school, district, and/or state levels. Furthermore, the author contends, research suggests that school suspension and expulsion may not be the best answers to discipline problems. David Hinojosa is national director of policy for Intercultural Development Research Association (IDRA), a nonprofit organization.

As you read, consider the following questions:

1. How did "zero-tolerance" policies affect school discipline, according to the viewpoint?
2. How can implicit bias lead to unfair treatment of some students?
3. Do schools as a whole benefit when suspension and expulsion are used as disciplinary tactics?

From a recent social media post showing a young high school girl being flung across the floor by a school resource officer (Ford, et al., 2015) to national reports of stark racial disparities in suspension rates, school discipline has resurfaced as a critical civil rights educational issue. Importantly, these events have forced many school boards, leaders and communities to take a second look at the systemic issues underlying poor disciplinary practices and the antiquated, ineffective policies around them.

Many of those ineffective policies stem from the adoption of zero tolerance measures over two decades ago (National Summit on Zero Tolerance, 2000). These policies initially targeted very specific, serious offenses involving weapons, drugs and acts of extreme violence. But they soon grew to include a number of minor, non-threatening offenses (Kang-Brown, et al., 2013). Not surprisingly, the proliferation of zero tolerance policies led to a spike in disciplinary actions, including suspensions.

In a 2015 report by the Center for Civil Rights Remedies, researchers found that "nearly 3.5 million public school students were suspended out of school at least once in 2011-12" (Losen, et al., 2015). This resulted in a loss of learning time estimated at 18 million days of instruction.

Even among discretionary offenses, a 2011 Texas study found that far fewer White male students (59 percent) had at least one discretionary violation compared to African American male students (83 percent) and Latino male students (74 percent). Similarly, 37 percent of White female students had at least one such violation compared to 70 percent of African American female students and 58 percent of Hispanic female students. (Fabelo, et al., 2011).

EQUITY IN SCHOOL DISCIPLINE

On July 30, 2018, House Bill 1541 allowed OSPI to address equity in student discipline and close opportunity gaps in learning across Washington state.

As educators, we differentiate instruction for students who struggle academically or learn in a different manner. It makes sense that educators use the same process for regulating behavior, as discipline is not a one-size-fits-all model. The new format is a prevention-based approach, schools must attempt to correct behavior before requiring disciplinary action. Following this format ensures fair and equitable practices across the state for all students.

The changes to federal and state laws are this: 1) Limit the use of exclusionary discipline in schools. 2) Minimize the impact of exclusionary discipline on students who are excluded. 3) Reduce disparities in the administration of student discipline.

Many educators have a false perception of the new discipline laws simply because they aren't well informed. I have heard many educators assume that the new rules mean two things. One, students perceived as "bad" can not be suspended for their behavior. And two, that those same "bad" students will be rewarded in hopes the rewards will change their behavior. This simply isn't true.

OSPI's Equity and Civil Rights Office officially advises schools to review the effectiveness of discipline and/or intervention strategies using a four-part model based on their school's discipline data.

• Plan: Analyze the data and identify root causes
• Do: Decide on a plan and implement
• Study: Evaluate and monitor progress
• Act: Adjust your plan, if necessary

In reviewing discipline policies schools should adjust their discipline rules if data shows little or no progress in student behavior.

"Equity in School Discipline," by Swan Eaton, Stories From School, December 26, 2019.

IDRA's South Central Collaborative for Equity—one of 10 federally-funded regional equity assistance centers—has assisted several schools in formulating more equitable student disciplinary policies and practices. Our experience shows that policies starting at the state level and continuing through to board policies, student codes of conducts and handbooks, and teacher manuals set the tone for student discipline (Cortez, 2009).

Factors that Lead to Unfair Discipline

When policies are vague, they give neither the educators nor the students sufficient notice of the expectations. When policies allow for discretionary referrals with a range of consequences, they often are not monitored and result in disproportionate offenses among racial groups. When policies governing the processes of disciplinary referrals are insufficient (such as very short timelines for contesting disciplinary actions), they can engender an atmosphere of mistrust and animosity among students of color—who are often the targets of discipline—which can lead to further disciplinary issues.

Research also suggests that the over-identification of students of color for disciplinary action may result from educators wrongly and unfairly disciplining minority students based on educators' implicit biases (Staats, 2014). In simple terms, implicit bias refers to "embedded stereotypes that heavily influence our decision-making without our conscious knowledge" (Godsil, et al., 2014), and virtually all people carry them. Typically, these are not biases we are consciously aware of and try to hide, but instead, are unconscious biases we hold that are likely fueled by stereotypes perpetrated in the media or beliefs passed along by parents, peers and other community members (Flannery, 2015).

For example, a White teacher may perceive a Black student's excited, inquisitive responses to a question as insubordination because the teacher unconsciously perceives the student as trying to disrupt the class. The teacher may then refer the student to the office, and such discretionary referrals can end up resulting in school suspension.

Teachers may also have lower expectations for students of color, leading to less praise and more disciplinary action from teachers (Rudd, 2014).

Reducing the Impact of Bias

The impact of these biases can be mitigated. First, teachers must become aware of their own biases (Flannery, 2015). In terms of discipline, a teacher can review his or her own referral records to determine racial disproportionalities, especially in terms of discretionary referrals. There also are tests available to help identify biases, such as Project Implicit's Hidden Bias Tests (2011).

Next, a teacher should reflect on his or her internal practices by asking questions, such as: "Who do I call on and how often?" "How do I seat students or group them?" "Do I truly value the differences among my students and if so, how?" "Do I have the same expectations for all my students?" (Flannery, 2015).

Affirmatively countering negative stereotypes that sustain biases with more accurate facts and perceptions can help lessen the influence of implicit bias (Flannery, 2015).

Racial disproportionality in student discipline and suspension must be addressed both at the policy and practice levels due to the substantial impact on student learning and social and emotional development. (Schools also should ensure their policies do not target students based on their disability, religious preference, and sex or gender.) Suspensions have been correlated to poor student outcomes, including decreased student achievement, lower graduation rates, higher dropout rates, suppressed student engagement, and future disciplinary exclusion (US Department of Education, 2015).

Contrary to popular belief, research shows a "negative relationship between the use of school suspension and expulsion and school-wide academic achievement, even when controlling for demographics, such as socioeconomic status" (APA, 2008).

Schools have the task of maintaining order and safety in the classroom while ensuring that all students learn and achieve. While it is no easy task, schools can begin to take steps or renew efforts in evaluating and correcting their student disciplinary policies and practices by committing to do the following, non-exhaustive actions (US Departments of Justice and Education, 2014).

- Examine disaggregated data by racial, gender, language, and disability subgroups at the teacher, grade, school and school district levels.
- Examine each type of discipline referral at the teacher, grade, school and school district levels.
- Examine data for students found to have been disciplined more than once to detect any patterns.
- If certain data are missing or not available, take steps to begin properly recording and maintaining the data.
- Create a task force that includes students, parents, teachers, counselors, support staff, administrators, board members, community members, and school resource/law enforcement officers (if required to assist with student discipline) to examine the data, school discipline policies, and supports and interventions.
- Survey students, teachers, counselors, support staff and the community about school climate.
- Conduct public hearings on the findings of the task force.
- Ensure school discipline policies and expectations are clear, fair and equitable for all students and student groups and that policies are founded on restorative justice and positive behavioral intervention support principles.
- Reduce the loss of learning time by limiting school suspensions to the most extreme behaviors and actions, such as inflicting serious bodily harm and possession of illegal weapons and illegal drugs that are accompanied by intent.
- Create a plan to improve student-teacher and teacher-parent communications and relationships.
- Develop a training and information program for students and community members that explains the school discipline

policies and student expectations in an age appropriate, easily understood manner.

- Provide training on implementing discipline policies in a nondiscriminatory manner and classroom management for all support staff, teachers, counselors, and administrators.
- Provide high quality training to teachers, support staff, counselors, and administrators on detecting implicit bias, developing cultural competency, and becoming aware of civil rights laws and federal guidance related to fair and effective school discipline.
- Consistently monitor and evaluate the implementation and impact of disciplinary practices to identify areas needing improvement and to ensure nondiscriminatory and equitable practices and policies are at work.
- At least annually, conduct a forum that provides students, support staff, teachers, counselors, and administrators the opportunity to discuss matters relating to discipline and provide input on the school's policies.

State leaders also can revisit their laws and regulations to ensure they are not explicitly or implicitly requiring, perpetuating or authorizing school discipline policies that result in unfair and racially disproportionate policies. Several resources are available to assist states and school districts, including IDRA's South Central Collaborative for Equity, regional equity assistance centers in your area, and the US Department of Education Office for Civil Rights.

Periodical and Internet Sources Bibliography

The following articles have been selected to supplement the diverse views presented in this chapter.

Alliance for Excellent Education, "Implicit Bias and Cultural Sensitivity Training," https://futureready.org/implementation -guide/implicit-bias-and-cultural-sensitivity-training/

American Institutes for Research, "Full-Service Community Schools provide students, their families, and the local community can receive academic, social, and health services, which can contribute to better educational outcomes for students," https:// www.air.org/project/full-service-community-schools-grant -evaluation-chicago-public-schools

Kristin Burnham, "'Cultural Responsiveness'" dismantles systemic bias and supports students from diverse cultural backgrounds," Northeastern University, July 31, 2020. https://www.northeastern .edu/graduate/blog/culturally-responsive-teaching-strategies/

Common Goal Systems Inc., "Schools should move away from grades and toward standards-based learning," https://www.teacherease .com/standards-based-grading.aspx

Department of Education, "Equity of Opportunity," https://www .ed.gov/equity

Swan Eaton, "Equity in School Discipline," The Center for Strengthening the Teaching Profession, December 26, 2019. https://storiesfromschool.org/equity-in-school-discipline/

Marcus Guido, "15 Culturally-Responsive Teaching Strategies and Examples + Downloadable List," Prodigy, September 14, 2017. https://www.prodigygame.com/in-en/blog/culturally-responsive -teaching/

Verna Lalbeharie, "Spotlight on Personalized Learning," American Institutes for Research, November 1, 2020. https://www.air.org /resource/spotlight-personalized-learning

Eric Saibel and Nathan Beach, "4 Strategies for Implementing Standards-Based Learning," George Lucas Educational Foundation, September 24, 2020. https://www.edutopia.org /article/4-strategies-implementing-standards-based-learning

For Further Discussion

Chapter 1

1. How do equity and equality differ, and which is more important? Why?
2. Is it important for a school system to be fair to all students? What would that look like?
3. Is it fair for schools to be supported by local taxes? What challenges result? What are other options?

Chapter 2

1. Boys and girls have different challenges in school, according to research. How can schools support equity for everyone, regardless of sex or gender?
2. Should schools support student health and wellness or only focus on academics? Why?
3. How can people make sure schools are safe and comfortable for everyone, regardless of sex, gender, or sexual orientation?

Chapter 3

1. Studies show many people do not think racism has a large effect on achievement. Do you agree? Why or why not?
2. Should teachers and school administrators be required to get antiracism training? Why or why not?
3. Should English language-learners get special accommodations? If so, what?

Chapter 4

1. What can schools do to support students who suffer from housing and security?
2. Children of low-income parents have fewer out of school opportunities than children of wealthier parents. What can

be done to make sure all young people have opportunities to identify and reach career goals?

3. How do rural schools compare to urban schools? What can be done to ensure students in each type of school get an equitable education?

Chapter 5

1. What are the advantages and disadvantages of various methods of personalized learning? Which do you think would work best for you?
2. Do you think culturally responsive teaching is important? Why or why not?
3. How would you design a school's disciplinary practices? Why?

Organizations to Contact

The editors have compiled the following list of organizations concerned with the issues debated in this book. The descriptions are derived from materials provided by the organizations. All have publications or information available for interested readers. The list was compiled on the date of publication of the present volume; the information provided here may change. Be aware that many organizations take several weeks or longer to respond to inquiries, so allow as much time as possible.

American Institutes for Research (AIR)

1400 Crystal Drive, 10th Floor
Arlington, VA 22202
(202) 403-5000
contact form: https://www.air.org/contact
website: www.air.org/

AIR's mission "is to generate and use rigorous evidence that contributes to a better, more equitable world." The website provides information on their research topics, including education.

The Brookings Institution

1775 Massachusetts Avenue NW
Washington, DC 20036
(202) 797-6000
email: communications@brookings.edu
website: www.brookings.edu/

The Brookings Institution is a nonprofit public policy organization. It researches and provides reports on topics such as global development and the US economy.

The Center on Reinventing Public Education (CRPE)

600 First Avenue
Seattle, WA 98104
(206) 685-2214
email: crpe@uw.edu
website: www.crpe.org/

CRPE is a center that hopes to find ways to make public education a system that prepares every student for the future. The website offers publications, information on current research, and a blog.

Education Writers Association (EWA)

1825 K Street NW, Suite 200
Washington, DC 20006
website: www.ewa.org/

EWA's mission is "to strengthen the community of education writers and improve the quality of education coverage to better inform the public." Website resources include articles on education, reporter guides, and tip sheets.

ETR (Education, Training & Research) Associates

5619 Scotts Valley Drive, Suite 140
Scotts Valley, CA 95066
(800) 620-8884
contact form: www.etr.org/about-us/contact/
website: www.etr.org/

ETR's mission is to "improve health and increase opportunities for youth, families and communities." The website discusses their projects, research, and programs.

Global Partnership for Education (GPE)

1850 K Street NW, Suite 625
Washington DC, 20006
(202) 458-0825
email: information@globalpartnership.org
website: www.globalpartnership.org

GPE focuses on access to education, inclusive education, and gender equality. The website provides links to fact sheets and other publications on these topics.

Head Start Early Childhood Learning and Knowledge Center (ECLKC)

US Department of Health & Human Services
330 C Street SW, Washington, DC 20201
(866) 763-6481
email: HeadStart@eclkc.info
website: eclkc.ohs.acf.hhs.gov/

Head Start provides grant funding and oversight to programs that promote school readiness of children from low-income families. Website topics include education and child development, family and community, and health.

Institute for Children, Poverty & Homelessness (ICPH)

36 Cooper Square
New York, NY 10003
(212) 358-8086
email: info@icphusa.org
website: www.icphusa.org/

ICPH, based in New York City, is a research organization focused on family homelessness. The website provides maps, infographics, and FAQs.

Intercultural Development Research Association (IDRA)

5815 Callaghan Road, Suite 101
San Antonio, TX 78228
(210) 444-1710
email: contact@idra.org
website: www.idra.org/

IDRA is a non-profit organization. Its mission is "to achieve equal educational opportunity for every child through strong public schools that prepare all students to access and succeed in college."

The Learning Policy Institute

1530 Page Mill Road, Suite 250
Palo Alto, CA 94304
(650) 332-9797
contact form: learningpolicyinstitute.org/contact-us
website: learningpolicyinstitute.org/

The Learning Policy Institute conducts research to improve education policy and practice. Website resources include fact sheets, infographics, and reports.

The Organisation for Economic Co-operation and Development (OECD)

2, rue André Pascal
75016 Paris
+33 1 45 24 82 00
contact form: https://www.oecd.org/contact/
website: www.oecd.org/

OECD is "an international organisation that works to build better policies for better lives." Priorities include fostering strong education. Click "education" under the topics tab for links to studies.

The United Nations University World Institute for Development Economics (UNU-WIDER)

Katajanokanlaituri 6 B
FI-00160 Helsinki
Finland
358-(0)9-615 9911
email: wider@wider.unu.edu
website: www.wider.unu.edu/

UNU-WIDER "provides economic analysis and policy advice with the aim of promoting sustainable and equitable development for all." The website provides information about the organization's programs, statistics, and publications.

University of the People (UoPeople)

595 E. Colorado Boulevard, Suite 623
Pasadena, CA 91101
(626) 264-8880
email: info@uopeople.edu
website: www.uopeople.edu/

University of the People is a nonprofit, tuition-free online university "dedicated to opening access to higher education globally." The website blog page has posts on college prep, careers, and online learning.

Waterford

4246 Riverboat Road
Taylorsville, UT 84123
(877) 299-7997
contact form: www.waterford.org/media-contact/
website: www.waterford.org/

Waterford supports "learning science, mentoring relationships, and innovative technologies to form community, school, and home programs that deliver excellence and equity for all learners." Learn about research and resources on the website.

Bibliography of Books

Kristyn Klei Borrero. *Every Student, Every Day: A No-Nonsense Nurturer Approach to Reaching All Learners*. Bloomington, IN: Solution Tree Press, 2018.

Olivia V. G. Clarke. *Black Girl, White School: Thriving, Surviving and No, You Can't Touch My Hair*. Columbus, OH: LifeSlice Media, 2020.

Antonia Darder. *Culture and Power in the Classroom: Educational Foundations for the Schooling of Bicultural Students (Series in Critical Narrative)*. Oxfordshire, UK: Routledge, 2015.

Kayren Gray. *The Road to Equity: The Five C's to Construct an Equitable Classroom*. Harker Heights , TX: MK Results, LLC, 2020.

Jessica Hannigan and John E. Hannigan. *Don't Suspend Me!: An Alternative Discipline Toolkit*. Thousand Oaks, CA: Corwin, 2016.

Felecia Carter Harris. *Gender and Education*. San Diego, CA: Cognella Academic Publishing, 2019.

Sonya Douglass Horsford. *Learning in a Burning House: Educational Inequality, Ideology, and (Dis)Integration*. New York, NY: Teachers College Press, 2011.

Baruti K. Kafele. *The Equity & Social Justice Education 50: Critical Questions for Improving Opportunities and Outcomes for Black Students*. Alexandria, VA: ASCD, 2021.

Nathan Maynard and Brad Weinstein. *Hacking School Discipline: 9 Ways to Create a Culture of Empathy and Responsibility Using Restorative Justice (Hack Learning Series)*. Cleveland, OH: Times 10 Publications, 2019.

Gholdy Muhammad. *Cultivating Genius: An Equity Framework for Culturally and Historically Responsive Literacy.* New York, NY: Scholastic Teaching Resources, 2020.

Tom Schimmer, Garnet Hillman, and Mandy Stalets. *Standards-Based Learning in Action: Moving from Theory to Practice (A Guide to Implementing Standards-Based Grading, Instruction, and Learning).* Bloomington, IN: Solution Tree, 2018.

Sydney Cail Snyder and Diane Staehr Fenner. *Culturally Responsive Teaching for Multilingual Learners: Tools for Equity.* Thousand Oaks, CA: Corwin, 2021.

Ann Wendle. *Women and Gender in Higher Education: Looking Forward, Looking Back (Culture and Society in Higher Education).* Gorham, ME: Myers Education Press, 2021.

Index

A

accountability policies, explanation of, 65

achievement gap, explanation of, 94

adverse childhood experiences (ACEs), 51

affirmative action, history of, 104–113

Alrubail, Rusul, 119–122

Amadeo, Kimberly, 53–59

America in Black and White, 105

Armour-Thomas, Eleanor, 111

Atlanta, public education in, 94

attention deficit hyperactivity disorder (ADHD), 49, 78

Austin Independent School District, 116–118

B

Baltimore, public education in, 94

Bell Curve, The, 105

Bhalotra, Sonia R., 72–76

Biden, Joe, 39

bisexual students, bullying of, 83–88

Brown v. Board of Education, 101

Burnham, Kristin, 170–175

Bush, George W., 31, 34, 36

C

Cardona, Miguel, 39

Carter, Prudence, 95

Caverly, Sarah, 114–118

Chatterji, Roby, 97–103

Childers-McKee, Cherese, 171–175

Children's Defense Fund, 134

Cimpian, Joseph, 64–71

Clarke, Damian, 72–76

community schools, 163

competency-based progression, 168

COVID-19 pandemic, 33–41, 95, 100, 101

Culturally Responsive Restorative Practices (CRRP) grant, 117

culturally responsive teaching, 163, 170–175

D

Darling-Hammond, Linda, 104–113

Department of Education, history of, 29

Detroit, public education in, 94

DeVos, Betsy, 32, 39

disciplinary policies, 180–186

downward-mobility effect, 57

Dreeben, Robert, 111

Dynarski, Mark, 135–143